The portraits on the cover have been
specially assembled to illustrate both the
wide timespan covered by this book and the
variety of ways in which monarchs have
been portrayed over the centuries.

These portraits are:

William I   coins
Henry III   effigy
Edward III   seal
Henry V   painting
Elizabeth I   painting
Charles I   miniature
George III   statuette
Queen Victoria   bust
Her Majesty the Queen   photograph

Royal Faces

900 YEARS OF BRITISH MONARCHY

LONDON
HER MAJESTY'S STATIONERY OFFICE

© Crown copyright 1977
First published 1977
Second impression 1977

ISBN 0 11 290209 X

HER MAJESTY'S STATIONERY OFFICE
Government Bookshops

49 High Holborn, London WC1V 6HB
13a Castle Street, Edinburgh EH2 3AR
41 The Hayes, Cardiff CF1 1JW
Brazennose Street, Manchester M60 8AS
Southey House, Wine Street, Bristol BS1 2BQ
258 Broad Street, Birmingham B1 2HE
80 Chichester Street, Belfast BT1 4JY

Government publications are also available through booksellers

The full range of Gallery publications is displayed and sold at the
National Portrait Gallery, London WC2H 0HE

Obtainable in the United States of America from Pendragon House Inc.
220 University Avenue, Palo Alto, California 94301

Text by Hugh Clayton
Picture selection and captions by
Mary Pettman and Richard Ormond
Designed by HMSO Graphic Design

Printed in England for Her Majesty's Stationery Office
by Ebenezer Baylis & Son Ltd, Worcester
Dd 290416   K184

ROYAL HOUSES

1066–1087	William I	*House of Normandy*
1087–1100	William II	
1100–1135	Henry I	
1135–1154	Stephen	
1154–1189	Henry II	*House of Plantagenet*
1189–1199	Richard I	
1199–1216	John	
1216–1272	Henry III	
1272–1307	Edward I	
1307–1327	Edward II	
1327–1377	Edward III	
1377–1399	Richard II	
1399–1413	Henry IV	*House of Lancaster*
1413–1422	Henry V	
1422–1461	Henry VI	
1461–1483	Edward IV	*House of York*
1483	Edward V	
1483–1485	Richard III	
1485–1509	Henry VII	*House of Tudor*
1509–1547	Henry VIII	
1547–1553	Edward VI	
1553–1558	Mary I	
1558–1603	Elizabeth I	
1603–1625	James I	*House of Stuart*
1625–1649	Charles I	
1649–1660	Interregnum	
1660–1685	Charles II	
1685–1688	James II	
1688–1702	William III	
1688–1694	Mary II	
1702–1714	Anne	
1714–1727	George I	*House of Hanover*
1727–1760	George II	
1760–1820	George III	
1820–1830	George IV	
1830–1837	William IV	
1837–1901	Victoria	
1901–1910	Edward VII	*House of Saxe-Coburg*
1910–1936	George V	*House of Windsor*
1936	Edward VIII	
1936–1952	George VI	
1952	Elizabeth II	

ACKNOWLEDGEMENTS

The following have kindly given permission for photographs to be reproduced in this book:

Her Majesty the Queen: Prince Albert p 46; Queen Victoria p 47

Archives Photographiques, Paris: Richard I p 11

Bildarchiv Foto Marburg: Edward II p 14

British Library Board: William II p 9; Henry I p 9; Henry II p 11 (Royal MS 20 A II fol 76); Richard I p 11; King John p 12 (Cotton MS Claudius D II fol 113); Henry V p 18 (Arundel MS 38 fol 37)

British Museum: Edward I p 5; Henry I p 9; Stephen p 10; Mary II p 37

Camera Press: Her Majesty the Queen p 55; Her Majesty the Queen and His Royal Highness the Duke of Edinburgh p 52; The Royal Family p 55; His Royal Highness the Prince of Wales p 7 and 54

The Archbishop of Canterbury and the Trustees of Lambeth Palace Library: Edward IV p 19

Central Press Photos: Her Majesty the Queen and Queen Elizabeth the Queen Mother p 52; Her Majesty the Queen p 54

Courtauld Institute of Art (Conway Library): Henry II p 10

Simon Wingfield Digby, Sherborne Castle: Elizabeth I p 27

The Worshipful Company of Fishmongers: Her Majesty the Queen p 53

A. F. Kersting: King John p 12

Musée du Louvre (Cliché des Musées Nationaux): Anne of Cleves p 24

The Mauritshuis, The Hague: Charles II p 35

Trustees of the National Gallery, London: Richard II p 16; Charles I p 5 and 33

National Monuments Records (Crown Copyright): Henry IV p 17

Phaidon Press: William I p 8

Popperfoto/United Press International: Her Majesty the Queen p 55

Public Record Office (Crown Copyright): Edward I p 13 (Memoranda Roll E 368/69m 54d)

Radio Times Hulton Picture Library: George VI and Family p 51

Thyssen-Bornemisza Collection: Henry VIII p 22

Victoria and Albert Museum (Crown Copyright): Henry VII p 21: Charles II p 34; James II p 35

Warburg Institute: Henry III p 13; Richard II p 16

The Dean and Chapter of Westminster: Edward III p 15; Henry VII p 21; Queen Anne p 38

Cover and title pages
A. H. Baldwin & Sons Ltd: William I
British Library Board: Edward III
Camera Press: Her Majesty the Queen

Introduction

Edward I *silver groat*

Charles I *by Sir Anthony Van Dyck*
(detail from the painting on page 33)

This book is intended to bring to life as vividly as possible the kings and queens who have reigned in England and Great Britain from William the Conqueror to the present day. The text has been written by Hugh Clayton, and should appeal to a wide audience, for it evokes the personalities of individual monarchs with great verve and insight, as well as describing the chief events of their reigns. It is often the small detail that pin-points a historical character, and the author strikes a fine balance between the general and the particular.

The illustrations are no less important. Books on kings and queens usually have no more than one illustration apiece, but here there are often four or five devoted to a single monarch, with full explanatory captions. It is instructive to be able to compare different images of the same figure, often widely separated by time, medium and style. Most of the portraits in the book come from the National Portrait Gallery; not only from its primary collection, but also from its vast archival store of prints and photographs. It was necessary to rely on outside sources for the medieval period, where portraits in the conventional sense of that word are very rare. Images of kings on seals and coins are purely symbolic, and it is not until the late fourteenth century that the tomb effigy assumes some likeness to the individual it commemorates. Certain very important portraits from other collections have also been included in the later sections, in order to give as comprehensive a view of the monarchy as possible. The Daily Herald Library, which the Gallery recently acquired, proved invaluable for photographs of the royal family in the present century.

We forget how much we owe to portraiture for giving a physical reality to our conception of kings and queens. However well known their lives may be, it is through the portraitist's eyes that we visualize them. Thomas Carlyle once said that a portrait was worth a handful of biographies, and one can see what he meant. The way a person looks and holds himself, his characteristics and idiosyncrasies, make an immediate impact, for which second-hand information is no substitute. In Holbein's Henry VIII we feel instinctively the power and menace of this autocrat, just as the melancholy features of Van Dyck's Charles I epitomize the courtly and romantic spirit of the Cavaliers.

Holbein and Van Dyck were great masters, whose work transcends the limiting conventions of court style. The state portrait, with its emphasis on traditional imagery, ermine robes, regalia and so forth, is often reduced to a formula in the hands of lesser artists. We see the king but not the individual. Sir Godfrey Kneller, for example, adapted his state portraits of successive monarchs from a limited range of patterns, and one can be forgiven for wondering whether a royal portrait by him represents James II, William III or George I. The mass production of copies of state portraits, for presentation purposes, adds to the problem. One usually sees Kneller not in the original, but at fourth hand in the work of some studio hack.

The dissemination of the royal image served an important propaganda function which monarchs were not slow to exploit. Images of state were designed to impress subjects with the power and majesty of their rulers. Holbein's great wall-painting of Henry VIII, Henry VII and their wives,

5

was a statement of a political and dynastic credo, underlining the king's new role as supreme head of church as well as state, following the breach with Rome. The elaborately symbolic portraits of his daughter, Elizabeth I, allegorize her as a national divinity, Gloriana in triumph, guiding her realm through the perils of internal dissension and foreign invasion. Charles I, riding out of a wood dressed in armour, in Van Dyck's great equestrian portrait in the National Gallery, exemplifies Stuart aspirations to imperial glory and absolute power.

The constitutional monarchy that followed the Restoration in 1660 could not sustain such grandeur, and the state portrait follows a more pedestrian path in terms of symbolism and ideology. Artistically, too, Van Dyck's successors show little originality, and it is not until the mid-eighteenth century that Allan Ramsay strikes an entirely new note in his elegantly rococo coronation portrait of George III, painted in a dazzling range of soft, powdery colours. George IV, his eldest son and successor, was passionately interested in the arts, and it is fitting that he should have been immortalized by the greatest portraitist of the age, Sir Thomas Lawrence, whose vitality and panache were complementary to his own. More recent state portraits have revealed a growing artificiality, as the outward forms and symbols of monarchy lose their significance. Portraiture is itself a traditional art in decline, and there are few memorable paintings of the royal family dating from the present century.

Though we tend to see kings and queens in terms of the pomp and circumstance of the state portrait, there are many other forms of royal image. The illustrations have been chosen to demonstrate this variety. Some of the most appealing representations of medieval kings are manuscript illustrations, like the delicate miniature of Henry V receiving a book from its author, Thomas Occleve, a rare contemporary image of this famous king. The remarkable personality of Elizabeth I inspired a cult of adoration among her courtiers, and this can be seen in the curious picture of her carried in procession, like a sumptuously dressed religious icon. Honthorst's picture of Charles I reading must be one of the first informal studies of a British monarch, and it offers an interesting contrast to Van Dyck's sad-eyed characterization of the king. Van Dyck's charming picture of the royal children introduces a new type of family group. In the eighteenth century, this tradition is carried a stage further in the conversation piece, brilliantly pioneered by Philip Mercier in his picture of Frederick, Prince of Wales, making music with his sisters. One can trace the subsequent development of such groups through the work of Zoffany in the later eighteenth century to Winterhalter in the nineteenth, and finally to James Gunn's Conversation Piece at the Royal Lodge, Windsor, painted as recently as 1950.

So far, discussion has been restricted to painting, but there are many other forms of representation. Sculpture, for example, has played an influential role, from the memorable twelfth-century tombs of Henry II and Richard I at Fontevrault Abbey, to the moving Renaissance bust of Henry VII, almost certainly by Pietro Torrigiano, and the brilliant baroque rendering of Charles II by Honoré Pelle. At a more popular level, there are full-length waxworks of various seventeenth and eighteenth-century monarchs, including Queen Anne, which are splendidly vivid, not to speak of medallic portraits, wax profiles and small statuettes. It is a commonplace that British art in its early days was dominated by a succession of foreigners, chief among them Holbein, Van Dyck and Lely. The most original contribution by artists born in this country during the sixteenth and seventeenth centuries was the art of miniature painting. Few will deny that

George III *studio of Allan Ramsay (detail from the painting on page 41)*

Elizabeth I *by Marcus Gheeraerts the Younger, c. 1592 (detail)*

6

Queen Victoria *by Sir Francis Chantrey, 1839*
(see drawing on page 45)

Charles, Prince of Wales
photograph by Karsh of Ottawa, 1975

Nicholas Hilliard's miniature of Elizabeth I or that of Charles II by Samuel Cooper are outstanding masterpieces in the art of portraiture, as profound in design and characterization as almost any contemporary work on a large scale.

For the last three or four centuries, the king's face has probably been better known through engravings, which reach a mass audience, than through paintings or other works of art. The print market becomes significant in the late sixteenth century, and there are some very important early examples, like the magnificent full-length of Elizabeth after Isaac Oliver, reproduced here. The introduction of mezzotint engraving led to much larger and more elaborate prints in the late seventeenth century. The work of John Smith is particularly fine, and he is shown here in a print of James II after Largillière. The satirical print is a product of the eighteenth century, reaching its peak in the work of James Gillray, who poured scorn and ridicule on the hapless George III and his dissolute sons.

Silhouette was another eighteenth-century invention, to be followed a generation or more later, in the 1840s, by the advent of photography. Here for the first time was an impartial standard against which to set the flattering impressions of the artist. Queen Victoria was eminently photogenic, and she took to the new invention with enthusiasm. If the camera recorded the truth about her plump figure and severe expression, it also communicated, far more powerfully than the paintbrush, her resolute force of character. The regal qualities of a monarch can be conveyed just as effectively by photography as by painting. Victorian photographs tend to be formal, but there are some telling studies of character, and some delightful family groups. The range of royal portraiture increased enormously, and, in an age of illustrated journalism, the royal family was recorded constantly in different situations and on different occasions.

This process has become even more marked in the present century. We see the royal family almost daily in the newspapers and on television, and our impression of them remains fluid and unformulated. It is impossible to say that this or that image has been more or less influential in recording the appearance of the monarch. This became very apparent when choosing the illustrations. It is feasible to establish some kind of priority with the portraits of earlier kings and queens, because they are limited in type and number. With twentieth-century monarchs, the choice is limitless, and for every painting or photograph selected there are hundreds of possible alternatives. Representation on this scale makes for comprehensiveness and complexity, but it also makes it harder for the artist or photographer to create an original work that will stand out from the repetitious stream of royal portraits.

In the hands of a great artist like Holbein or Van Dyck, we see the king set down definitively for all time. No such certainty of vision can exist in an age dominated by photography and film, when one impression of appearance is constantly qualified by another. Perhaps in the future portraiture will emerge from the doldrums, and the monarchy once more find permanent record in the realm of art.

Richard Ormond
Deputy Keeper
National Portrait Gallery

William 1

Born 1027, reigned 1066–1087

The man who led the most recent successful armed invasion of England was known to his Norman contemporaries as William the Bastard. His father was Duke Robert of Normandy, a descendant of Vikings who may have raided Scotland a century earlier, and his mother was a tradesman's daughter. When William was barely seven years old his father went on crusade to the Holy Land and disappeared on the return journey.

The Norman magnates of the eleventh century were a ruthless and turbulent breed, but William showed, through years of fighting for his inheritance, that he could be as ferocious as any and more cool-headed than most. He grew into a stern, efficient but illiterate warrior whose hallmark was a calculated mixture of mercy and cruelty. On campaign in Normandy and England he would devastate one strongpoint in order to cow the next into surrender.

While William strengthened his possessions in Normandy, Edward the Confessor, King of England, failed to subdue his own most powerful subjects. He married the sister of Harold of Wessex, but remained childless and probably named William of Normandy as his heir. It is also probable that Harold was induced to accept William's claim. By Christmas 1065, Edward lay ill, prophesying disaster for his kingdom. It is certain that William felt cheated when Harold accepted the English crown from the Witan early in 1066.

William was not the only invader of England in 1066. Harold had first to march against a vast host from Norway which penetrated as far as York. He showed his mettle as a commander by destroying it within a week. William landed in Sussex a few days later and had enough time to prepare his forces before Harold could hasten southwards. The Battle of Hastings began on an October morning, and for some hours neither side was able to inflict crippling damage on the other. At one point William had to exhibit himself to the Normans in order to quash a rumour that he had been killed. In the afternoon his soldiers broke the discipline of the English line by feigning retreats that lured away small bands of pursuers. It was then that Harold fell, according to tradition with an arrow through one eye.

William I *by an unknown artist*
One of a set of portraits of early kings and queens that has apparently always hung at Hornby Castle, seat of the Dukes of Leeds. These sets, reflecting an interest in historical portraiture, were hung in the long galleries of sixteenth-century country houses. The Leeds set of sixteen portraits was begun in the 1590s and was probably produced by different workshops. The portrait of William dates from around 1620–30, and appears to derive from a woodcut of 1597. It has no authenticity as a contemporary likeness.

The kingdom of England was William's for the taking. His victory was one of the most significant in European history.

There was no single rallying point for the English after the battle, but the Conqueror faced many rebellions. His most durable opponents were Waltheof of Huntingdon and Hereward the Wake.

William's possessions bestrode the Channel and he spent much of his reign outside England. But he brought lasting change to the country by implanting an alien aristocracy and law, and by imposing his own brand of feudalism which ensured his dominating position up to the day of his death. His greed was notorious and in his last years he commissioned a detailed survey of the resources of his kingdom so that he could assess it for tax. The resulting Domesday Book is one of the most impressive administrative legacies of the Middle Ages.

William died on campaign, troubled by the rivalry of his sons. He won power that made him a martinet, but which would have made tyrants of most other men.

William I *silver penny*
Coins are among the commonest objects on which one finds a representation of the king's head, from Anglo-Saxon times onwards. The treatment of the features is, however, extremely crude and diagrammatic, and these coin images are in no sense portraits as we understand the word. This particular example was minted by the moneyer Wulfmaer at Romney, from a die probably designed by the king's goldsmith, Theodoric, around 1068.

William I *detail from the Bayeux Tapestry*
The Bayeux Tapestry tells the story of the Norman Conquest in a thin strip more than seventy metres (seventy-six yards) long. Its survival, in remarkably good condition, is little short of miraculous, and nothing else like it is known. The tapestry is thought to have been commissioned by William's brother, Bishop Odo of Bayeux, and it tells the story of the events leading up to the Battle of Hastings in a lively and dramatic style, full of detail about contemporary life. The detail reproduced here shows William the Conqueror acknowledging Harold's oath of allegiance, after the latter's shipwreck in France and before the death of Edward the Confessor.

William II   Henry I

Born *c.* 1056, reigned 1087–1100

The bonds of government which William the Conqueror had tied so carefully were loosened after his death by the rivalry of his sons. Robert, the oldest, had actually wounded his father in battle. He resented being bequeathed Normandy while one of his brothers was awarded England. King William II, nicknamed Rufus because of his red hair, was as ruthless and as greedy as his father. But while the Conqueror was pious the younger William eschewed Christianity and despised priests. William I had nine children but William II had none. Some say that he was a flamboyant homosexual. He was fiercely condemned by medieval chroniclers and it has even been suggested that he worshipped pagan gods. However, William was a resourceful commander, and his feats gradually won support away from his disgruntled brother. His incessant need to raise money through taxes aroused the resentment of his subjects and led to a quarrel with the church that terrified Anselm, his Archbishop of Canterbury.

William was an enthusiastic hunter and his game was jealously preserved in the royal forests. He died in one of them by a single bowshot, perhaps assassinated by a fellow hunter connected with his younger brother, Prince Henry.

William II   *wax seal*
The image of the king on seals is more elaborate than that on the coinage, but no more revealing as to individual likeness or character. Medieval seals follow a traditional design, showing the king enthroned in majesty on one side, and usually on horseback as a military leader on the reverse or counter-seal. As a patent of authority the seal has always been of the greatest importance, and is to be found attached to charters and official documents.

Henry I   *silver penny*
The coinage changed several times during Henry's reign, due probably to the need to check its quality. This is an example of the fifth type, minted by Wulfgar at London. The king is shown with a crown and sceptre.

Born 1068, reigned 1100–1135

William the Conqueror bequeathed land to two of his sons and money to Henry, the youngest. The prince spent his youth in conspiracies that showed him to be the equal of any of his family in sly and effective diplomacy. When William Rufus was King of England Henry took the side of their elder brother, Robert, and pushed one of William's supporters to his death from a tower. Four years later he joined William against Robert. When William died childless Henry first secured the royal treasury at Winchester and then proceeded hastily to his coronation.

Long after his death chroniclers called Henry I Beauclerc, the Scholar, because he encouraged men of learning at court. He had few pretensions to scholarship himself and was probably illiterate like his father. The stability which he brought to England encouraged trade and municipal growth while some of the most famous medieval monasteries in the country were founded in his reign. The ill feeling which William Rufus had brought to relations between Church and State was reduced and the new king did much more than his father and brother to reconcile his Norman and English sub-

Henry I   *wax seal*
This is an example of Henry's fourth seal. It differs little in design from the seals of his predecessors, showing the linear style typical of Romanesque art. The king enthroned in majesty has been one of the most potent images associated with the monarchy from earliest times.

jects. The Normans sneered when he married a woman who was descended from Alfred the Great through the King of Scots. But Henry was not to be driven from his aim of securing the succession; neither was he diverted from several mistresses who bore him numerous children.

The second half of his reign brought Henry to the greatest test of his life. The heir apparent, Prince William, was drowned when the White Ship was wrecked on a voyage from Normandy to England, in 1120. The king's harsh will enabled him to rally quickly and marry his reluctant daughter, Matilda, to Geoffrey, Count of Anjou. It was a skilful match because the counts of Anjou had been among the most dangerous enemies of the dukes of Normandy.

Although Henry was capable of great generosity he kept an iron grasp on the leading men of the realm and particularly on those portions of their revenues which were due to the Crown. He also created travelling justices, a noteworthy piece of devolution of judicial power, and was remembered for encouraging mercantile guilds. By stifling the forces for disorder, the last of the Norman kings of England enabled the country to gain stability and strength.

Stephen

Henry 11

Born *c.* 1097, reigned 1135–1154

Henry I left all of his possessions to his daughter, Matilda, but Stephen was the first to gain the crown. He had some early diplomatic successes but soon alienated some of his most powerful supporters and showed that he could not control the ambition of the leading men of the kingdom.

Stephen was a grandson of William the Conqueror, and by the time of his accession had become one of the most extensive landowners in England. Historians have dismissed him as a failure who allowed the country to suffer 'nineteen long winters' of baronial disorder. But they disagree about whether his weakness came about because he was shallow and timid or because his was a noble and generous temperament that could not descend to the level at which diplomacy was practised in the twelfth century. There is no doubt that he was splendid in battle, but he was inadequate in politics.

Stephen *silver penny*
The quality of the coinage declined during Stephen's reign, no doubt a reflection of the state of almost incessant civil war. This example was minted by William of Carlisle.

Henry II and Eleanor of Aquitaine
tomb effigies in Fontevrault Abbey, Poitou
The effigies of Henry II, his wife Eleanor of Aquitaine, Richard I, and Isabella of Angoulême, queen of King John, are the earliest surviving sculptures of English monarchs. It shows the strength of their attachment to their Continental possessions that they should choose to be buried in what was then Anjou; their tombs make a memorable impression in the gaunt setting of this great Romanesque abbey. There is little doubt that the two kings and queens are represented as they were carried to burial, but the circumstances in which the effigies were made remain unknown. It is unlikely that they were intended as likenesses, but rather as symbolic images of dead monarchs.

Born 1133, reigned 1154–1189

When Henry II began his long and active reign, there was an English Pope, Adrian IV, at Rome. He entrusted the king with the conquest of Ireland and the reform of its church, and a later Pope made Henry overlord of that country. Henry added it to a varied and turbulent empire that included England and half of what is now France.

Henry, first of the Plantagenet kings, was a burly, cultivated and foul-tempered warrior with penetrating eyes, whose astonishing energy enabled him to keep a vast dominion intact for most of his reign. The son of that Matilda whose claim to the English throne Stephen had brushed aside, he was little more than fourteen when he launched his first attack on England. It petered out farcically in Wiltshire, but long before he came of age he had become Stephen's most dangerous adversary.

Henry I had claimed the crown in haste, but his grandson felt secure enough to linger in Normandy for two months after Stephen's death. Henry's marriage to Eleanor of Aquitaine, only a few weeks after her match with Louis VII of France had been nullified, brought him possessions that stretched to the Pyrenees. His vigour was exceptional, for as well as garrisoning Ireland he reformed the chaotic government of Brittany and strengthened his officials' power to control ambitious magnates in Normandy. All Europe felt his influence, and brilliant men were attracted to his service. His most lasting administrative changes were in England where he contained the martial ardour of the barons by dismantling their castles, discouraging tournaments and accepting cash instead of knight service. He encouraged the growth of a militia outside the retinues of his most powerful vassals.

Henry's legal reforms were even more significant, since his reign saw the widespread use in primitive form of the jury system and the first codification of case law by judges themselves. But in popular memory all this king's achievements pale beside the clash with Thomas Becket, Archbishop of Canterbury, whom Henry had first raised to high office. As young men they were cheerful comrades in the sports of their time but Becket as Primate became a sincere and immovable champion of Church against State. If men in holy orders were charged with criminal offences they were tried in ecclesiastical courts where penalties were light. Henry wanted them to face the king's law, and was unmollified when Becket tried to appease him by introducing harsher sentences in Church courts. The king hounded his old friend mercilessly until the famous day when, while in Normandy, he cursed his knights for their weakness in allowing a single cleric to defy their lord. He was appalled when four of them murdered the archbishop in his cathedral, and he did penance for their crime.

Richard I

Henry II arguing with Thomas à Becket
A manuscript illumination from the
'Chronicle of England by Peter of Longtoft',
a history of England up to the death of
Edward I, in French verse. The illumination

Born 1157, reigned 1189–1199

History has been kind to the achievement of this king, who spent most of his reign outside England. Legend has made Richard the Lion Heart a hero who returned from distant wars to undo the abuses and cruelty of the clique that followed his younger brother, John. But the Lion Heart's main interest was in crusading adventures to the Holy Land, and England concerned him solely as a source of funds.

Richard had passed his thirtieth year when his father, Henry II, died. The two had been at loggerheads for years, and Richard had concentrated on pacifying those of his father's dominions which were most remote from England. He was an inspiring and skilful commander whose arrogance was often tempered by mercy. He excelled in the arts of war, and his Château Gaillard, one of the earliest concentric castles in Western Europe, was a masterpiece of fortification. But though his prowess in the field aroused fear and wonder he was no statesman. He sold offices in England to help finance the Third Crusade, on which he defeated Saladin, paused within sight of Jerusalem and tried to establish a permanent Christian settlement in the Holy Land.

Henry II faced his greatest worldly test at the age of forty when a rebellion by two of his sons was taken as the signal for revolt all over his empire. He beat them all but did not survive a more powerful alliance fifteen years later. He surrendered, and asked who had conspired against him; his beloved son John headed the list, and Henry died two days later.

is an interesting illustration of the conflict between Henry and Becket, reflecting the struggle between Church and State, but as a representation of the two men it is entirely formalized.

Richard I *wax seal*
An example of the reverse or counter-seal of
Richard's second seal, showing him on
horseback.

The king died in his prime, while attempting to storm the fortress of Chaluz, after a shoulder wound from a crossbow bolt became septic.

Richard I and Eleanor of Aquitaine
tomb effigies in Fontevrault Abbey, Poitou
Richard I asked to be buried at the feet of
his father, Henry II.

Henry II *silver penny*
Minted by Godwin of Worcester, and an
example of the so-called 'short-cross' issue,
introduced in 1180. On the later 'long-cross'
coinage, the four arms of the cross on the
reverse reached to the edge of the coins, to
discourage clipping or trimming.

John

Henry III

Born 1167, reigned 1199–1216

Tradition has exalted the memory of Richard I and denigrated that of his brother John. Although the recesses of his character remain mysterious, John was certainly not a cruel prince whose agents were free to torment the subjects of the absent Lion Heart; that is too simple a view of his complex and erratic personality. Moreover, the popular idea that he was a shifty and feckless king who reluctantly confirmed the liberties of his subjects at Runnymede in 1215 is false. Magna Carta was meant to advance the ambitions of those who already had the greatest power after the king.

John was despised in his lifetime for losing Normandy, but he had some military successes: in 1209 he won hostages from the King of Scots; in 1210 he won the submission of most of the Irish chieftains, and a year later he chastised Gwynedd. But he never beat his greatest rival, Philip Augustus of France.

He quarrelled with Innocent III, one of the most implacable of medieval Popes, who intended that Stephen Langton should become Archbishop of Canterbury when the primacy became vacant. John protested that his right of patronage was being flouted and that anyway Langton was unacceptable. The Pope placed England under an interdict so that no services could be held and nobody married or buried by the clergy. The king replied by issuing an order for the confiscation of the property of men in holy orders, some of whom were very wealthy indeed. Later, the same Pope reprimanded Langton for taking part in the demands that led to Magna Carta.

John was an agitated and temperamental monarch who had been pampered as a boy and then denied the success he had been brought up to expect. In some ways a conscientious ruler, John enjoyed hearing legal cases himself and made a sincere effort to restore the standard of the silver coinage. He was a careful commander-in-chief who created a fleet of war galleys and reorganized the local levies in the shires. He was also something of a scholar and enjoyed his large library.

John died on a feverish and desperate flight from a French invasion of England, on which his treasure was lost in the Wash, in East Anglia.

Born 1207, reigned 1216–1272

When King John died, half of his kingdom was occupied by a foreign army that enjoyed English support, and his heir was only nine years old. But the young Henry III had strong support and the French invasion was stemmed.

The new king was to reign for more than fifty years, and grow into a devout and scholarly man with an impressive presence that should have made him respected in castle and cloister. But Henry was flawed by ambition that exceeded his ability, and by a petty and vindictive spirit. He was one of those rulers of England whose fixed and lofty concept of the status of the sovereign hardened them against the aspirations of their most powerful subjects. John's loss of Normandy and the English possessions to the south nagged at his son for years and Henry launched two attempts at conquest. Both failed and he emerged with a portion of what is now south-west France.

Henry's protectors had rallied support at the beginning of his reign by re-stating Magna Carta, but he later appeared to his barons to have deserted its principles. He enjoyed French culture and society and alarmed Englishmen, after his marriage to Eleanor of Provence, by importing incompetent and insensitive advisers from courts overseas. An uncle of the new queen was made Archbishop of Canterbury, in which office he was remembered as the most hated man in the kingdom. Simon de Montfort, another arrival with

King John   *tomb effigy in Worcester Cathedral (detail)*
This marble effigy, one of the masterpieces of the Purbeck school of sculptors, was probably executed between 1225 and 1230. The strongly modelled squat head, supported by two bishops, has great force, but there is no evidence that it records John's appearance. Indeed, the features conform to a pattern found in other sculptures by the Purbeck school. The effigy was originally coloured.

King John   A charming miniature of the king hunting, from the manuscript 'De Rege Johanne', an account of his reign in Latin.

Edward I

the queen's party, was married in secret to a sister of the king. Meanwhile, the English barons resented the growth of this powerful clique of alien advisers, and Henry's intransigence helped to push the country towards civil war. The king had alienated even de Montfort, who summoned an assembly of representatives from the shires which he called a 'speaking', or, in his native French, a 'parlement'. That assembly grew later into the House of Commons.

By the 1260s an accumulation of grievances had built up against the king, and these now included his determination to pursue, at the taxpayer's expense, a family claim to the crown of Sicily. De Montfort raised the standard of revolt. At first he was successful and the king was defeated and captured. Then Prince Edward managed to set him free and together they beat de Montfort at Evesham in 1265. The great statesman was killed, but Henry was more restrained in his government afterwards.

His most enduring monuments were some of the finest buildings of his age, for this king was a dedicated patron of ecclesiastical architecture.

Henry III   *tomb effigy in Westminster Abbey by William Torel (detail)*
Commissioned by Henry's son, Edward I, together with an effigy of Edward's wife, Eleanor of Castile, in 1291, as part of a programme of dynastic glorification. No doubt Edward was anxious to rival the French royal tombs in St Denis. The effigies were executed by the king's goldsmith, William Torel, and they are the first full-length figures in English sculpture to be cast in bronze.

Born 1239, reigned 1272–1307

The reign of this wise and martial king saw the start of the flowering of medieval England. Edward made an early start to his adventurous career by entering public life at twelve and marrying at fourteen. He was embarrassed by the behaviour of his father, Henry III, but remained unshakeably loyal to him. Edward was asked, after the old king's death, why he had grieved more about that than over the death of his own small son. He answered that a son could be replaced, while a father could not.

Edward came to the throne in the prime of life, tall, broad-shouldered, with legs that made him a secure horseman and earned him the nickname Longshanks. He showed military promise early, and in the campaign against Simon de Montfort won an engagement with a simple trick after capturing the rebel's son: Edward ordered his men to advance on the father with the son's banners and to unfurl their own at the last moment. When Henry died, Edward was abroad, recovering from a wound received while on crusade. Other nations left the expedition as it was about to embark and Edward led an English contingent which relieved Acre and took Nazareth. He was grazed by a poisoned dagger as he beat off a would-be assassin.

Edward I is best remembered for those attempts at conquest within the British Isles, one of which earned him the title Hammer of the Scots. But first he turned to Wales where, before he came of age, his lands had been devastated by Welshmen who resented the designs of English barons on their independent principality. A final rebellion in 1282 was crushed in a skirmish in which a soldier from Salop killed the leader of a Welsh raiding party. Only when he examined the body did he discover that his victim was Llywelyn, the last independent Prince of Wales. His title was bestowed on Edward's son and has since been held by the eldest son of the sovereign, including Prince Charles today.

The king's failure to subjugate Scotland was a tribute to the determination and resilience of its people. William Wallace was an inspiring leader who ravaged Cumbria until he was captured, executed and had his head impaled on London Bridge. Edward won a decisive victory at Falkirk where he led his army even

Edward I
A drawing of the king in profile, with the arms of England emblazoned on his costume, carrying a staff with a bird on the top. It comes from the Memorandum Roll, one of the records of royal administration, and dates from 1297–98.

after two of his ribs had been broken by a kick from a horse. He then set up a council to govern Scotland and tried to introduce sheriffs in the regions there. But the Scots were more determined to resist foreign occupation than were the English to impose it and they remained determined to resist even after their most famous leader, Robert the Bruce, had been captured and his brother executed.

Edward was a vigorous administrator at home and introduced important statutes about the transfer of land. He was deeply saddened by the death of his wife at forty-five after bearing him thirteen children. The king himself died full of apprehension about his son's ability to complete the conquest of the Scots.

13

Born 1284, reigned 1307–1327

A distasteful and mysterious chapter in English history began when this king warily mounted the throne with a legacy of enormous debt and unattainable designs on Scotland. One of his first acts was to recall Piers Gaveston, the companion of his boyhood, whom Edward I had expelled from court. Edward II was infatuated with Gaveston and rewarded him with a lucrative earldom. The favourite, far from appreciating that nothing but royal protection lay between him and baronial vengeance, strutted vainly in the king's entourage to the disgust of the nobility. Edward married the French king's daughter, Isabella, who began by hating Edward's favourites and ended by gladly helping to destroy her husband.

Edward could neither save Gaveston nor enforce the claim of the English Crown to rule Scotland. The favourite was captured by barons who gave him an assurance of safe conduct and then beheaded him. Scotland was lost at the Battle of Bannockburn in 1314, where a vast but cramped English force was destroyed after hours of furious combat by a smaller army of Scots. The king, who had plunged into the fray at first, accusing the more cautious of the nobles of cowardice, galloped away with a few followers. Edward was eventually deposed, bundled away to a dungeon in Gloucestershire and killed in bestial fashion.

Edward II   *tomb effigy in Gloucester Cathedral (detail)*
Commissioned by Edward III in the 1330s as a memorial to his father, who had been brutally murdered in Berkeley Castle. Edward II enjoyed the status of a martyr and his tomb was the focus of a popular cult.

Edward III   *by an unknown artist*
Like the portrait of William I, this is one of the Leeds set of early kings and queens, executed in the early seventeenth century. The artist appears to have derived the head from the tomb effigy.

Edward III

Born 1312, reigned 1327–1377

The long reign of Edward III began uncertainly and ended in squalor, but the years between formed a splendid pageant of chivalry, full of great victories and magnificent tournaments. The king swore at one feast that he would create in England a great assembly of the flower of knighthood, after the Round Table of King Arthur. He kept his pledge in 1348 by founding the Order of the Garter. But Edward's campaigns faced a constraint that seems never to have worried anyone at Camelot, lack of funds. Once he had to pawn the Crown jewels and later to leave an earl in Flanders as collateral for his debts. He ruined some of the great banking houses of Florence by delaying repayments on gigantic loans. The great aim of his life was to win the throne of France, which he claimed through his mother, Isabella, the daughter of a French king.

Before he could deal with France, Edward had to tame his mother, who when he acceded to the throne of England at the age of fourteen, had determined to direct the government.

She took a lover from the English nobility and the pair behaved with outrageous arrogance. Their unpopularity reached its height when they propelled the young king into a pact with the Scots in which Robert Bruce was recognized as an independent monarch. At the age of eighteen Edward staged a coup to remove his objectionable guardians. He surprised them by entering a castle through a secret passage, detained the amorous earl for an early execution and consigned his mother to a comfortable and powerless retirement in East Anglia.

Edward was strong, imposing and energetic. He supported the poet Chaucer, and, three centuries after the Norman Conquest, he was one of the first English kings to speak the native language. (French was the first tongue of the nobility of medieval England.) Edward was acutely conscious of his kingdom's dependence on foreign trade and shocked his subjects by encouraging the immigration of first-class Flemish weavers.

After the French had ravaged the English ports Edward tried to form a great alliance against them. He could not wait to start the war and offered one of his daughters in marriage to the sons of two

Edward III *tomb effigy in Westminster Abbey (detail)*
Executed around 1377–80 and cast in copper gilt. The name of the sculptor is not known, but the style of the effigy reflects French influence. The head appears to derive from the wooden effigy also in Westminster Abbey, and it therefore reveals what Edward actually looked like, although the interpretation is formal and stylized.

European potentates at once. The Hundred Years War began in earnest with a great naval victory for England. When Edward managed to invade France he was shadowed by a vast French army which in 1346 he defeated with triumphant skill at Crécy. Ten years later, at Poitiers, the French king was captured after another English victory, but England was too weak to subdue his subjects. Military success in France and the loot that flowed home in its train diverted Englishmen from problems at home. There were many in Edward's reign, including the fearsome plague called the Black Death in 1348–49; the king's main concern was to ensure that the sharp drop in the number of farm labourers which resulted did not lead to higher wages.

Edward retained his popularity in England as long as his much-loved wife Philippa lived, but after her death in 1369 he fell under the influence of unscrupulous favourites, including a mistress who completely demoralized him.

Edward III *wooden effigy in Westminster Abbey, probably by Stephen Hadley (detail)*
According to the wardrobe accounts, Hadley was paid for 'an image in likeness' of a king soon after Edward's death in 1377, and this was placed on his coffin in St Paul's during the funeral ceremony. The head of the effigy may derive from a death-mask, and the slightly twisted expression of the mouth on the right seems to record the effects of a stroke Edward is known to have suffered before he died.

Richard II

Born 1367, reigned 1377–1399

Historians are not quite sure what to make of Richard II. They cannot decide whether he was a peace-loving and unlucky king destroyed by baronial greed for power, or a deceitful and imperious weakling who graduated from despotism to paranoia. Certainly, the struggle between Richard and the barons should not be seen as an early attempt to bring democracy to English government. The two sides reached their greatest unity when they turned on the common folk who had joined the Peasants' Revolt.

Richard was nine when he acceded and had to be carried on his tutor's shoulder through a long and lavish coronation. The ceremony ended with the king's champion, splendidly armed, standing at the door of Westminster Abbey and daring any opponent to step forward. Richard was only fourteen when heavy taxation against which there was no appeal led to a ferocious uprising in southern England, in 1381, which came to be known as the Peasants' Revolt. The

Richard II *by an unknown artist,*
'The Wilton Diptych'
This famous diptych, showing Richard being presented to the Virgin and Child by his patron saints, is a unique and fascinating work of art of the highest quality. It is not known why or when it was painted, and many of its visual allusions remain obscure. The image of Richard agrees reasonably well with other known portraits and it was either executed during his lifetime or soon after his death.

royal party sheltered in the Tower of London until Richard decided to confront some of the rebels in person. A resentful and ill-disciplined crowd faced the king and a few nervous followers, and when the rebel leader was stabbed the mob prepared to charge. Richard instantly darted forward alone and declared that he would lead them. The rebels faltered and were pacified with promises that nobody intended to keep.

When Richard reached manhood he took over the reins of government, and over the years ruled with increasing absoluteness, getting deeply involved in savage disputes with nobles who despised him. Meanwhile he set new standards in luxury at court, but at the same time encouraged poetry and music, and was among those who patronized Geoffrey Chaucer.

It is not certain how Richard died, only that he was brusquely deposed and confined in Pontefract Castle by his cousin, Henry Bolingbroke, who became Henry IV.

Richard II *tomb effigy in Westminster Abbey by Nicholas Broker and Godfrey Prest (detail)*
Richard was the first English monarch to sit for his portrait in the modern sense of the word. Sensitive and artistic by temperament, he was culturally far in advance of his time. This bronze effigy was executed during Richard's lifetime, between 1395 and 1397, together with a companion effigy of his queen, Anne of Bohemia, who died in 1394. Comparison between the effigy and the two painted images of Richard provides a good idea of his delicate, somewhat effeminate features.

Richard II *copy of the painting in Westminster Abbey*
The original was executed during Richard's lifetime. Although the figure has the priestly qualities of a religious icon, the head possesses a pronounced sense of character. It is a measure of the rarity of this painting, and the Wilton Diptych, that no other painted portraits of kings and queens are known before the late fifteenth century, and that one has to wait for Holbein's *Henry VIII* for a comparable full-length.

Henry IV

Henry V

Born 1366, reigned 1399–1413

There must have been moments when Henry of Bolingbroke, Duke of Lancaster, regretted elbowing his cousin, Richard II, off the throne of England. He was the elder by little more than a year and had carried a symbolic sword at Richard's coronation. His ancestry and marriage brought Henry vast landholdings. He was short, bearded, impatient and adventurous and spent some of Richard's reign on lavish tours of Europe and the Middle East, travelling like a prince with heralds to announce his passing and with gifts to make his visit remembered. When Richard was in the ascendant he tried to deprive Henry of his lands. Henry came from the north to claim them, saying that he did not want the crown. But he soon took it when Richard failed to rally support, and thus became the first Lancastrian king of England.

Although the Scots and French were persistent in their enmity towards the new regime, the greatest danger to it arose in Wales, from one of the great patriots of the principality. This was Owain Glyndŵr, whose cause became all the more formidable when he cemented an alliance with nobles who thought themselves inadequately rewarded for helping Henry to seize power. The rebellion was crushed and Glyndŵr eventually disappeared. Henry 'Hotspur' Percy, leader of the English faction that fought with him, was executed.

Thereafter, the king sank into illness of one kind and another, and by the time of his death the executive power was already in the hands of his son, Henry of Monmouth.

Born 1387, reigned 1413–1422

Legends that grew around the memory of Henry V after his death have made historians suspicious of him. They now doubt that he spent his youth in dissipation and then became stern and upright when he took the throne. They do not believe that the French replied to his dynastic claims with a box of tennis balls and the advice that he should grow up. They hold that he was always austere and single-minded and that there was nothing frivolous about his diplomatic correspondence with France. He claimed to be king of that country as well as of England and was such a magnificent soldier that he came closer than anyone in English history to repaying the Norman Conquest in kind.

The king enforced his claim on France with an army of at least ten thousand men. A third died in an early siege, but Henry insisted on pressing forward through 150 miles of enemy country to the English possession of Calais. The weary and apprehensive English met a much larger and more confident French force at Agincourt. A ponderous advance by heavily-armed Frenchmen was shattered by hails of arrows from hundreds

Henry V *by an unknown artist*
From a set of kings and queens produced in the workshops of Tudor artists. Although clearly posthumous, the image may derive from a contemporary likeness of some kind. The profile pose suggests that the original may have been a votive picture, like the Wilton Diptych of Richard II.

Henry IV and Joanna of Navarre
tomb effigies in Canterbury Cathedral (detail)
This joint tomb shows the technical virtuosity achieved by the late alabaster carvers; like the tomb of Edward II, it was originally coloured and gilded. The tomb was opened in 1832, and the head and beard of Henry's corpse were found to be in a remarkably good state of preservation, suggesting that the effigy was a reasonably accurate likeness. It is the only certain portrait of the king.

Henry VI

Born 1421, reigned 1422–1461 and 1470–1471

The infant who succeeded Henry V faced a crushing inheritance. England was exhausted and overtaxed as a result of pursuing unattainable designs on France, and the nobility was restless at home. Henry VI was no warlord; in fact, some contemporaries dismissed him as a helpless nincompoop. He was almost fanatical in religious observance and was absent at prayer during one of his party's most decisive defeats because it was Palm Sunday. He was an enthusiastic patron of learning and founded King's College, Cambridge. He also founded Eton and delighted in meeting the boys there. But he was too important to the dynastic rivalries of Lancaster, of which he was the figurehead, and York to be left alone. He was tossed about helplessly in the Wars of the Roses which broke out in 1455, and had constantly to be prodded into action by his passionate and ambitious queen, Margaret of Anjou. Henry's followers were disgusted when he proclaimed the Duke of York heir to the throne in preference to his own son. He was successively toppled and restored by Warwick, the 'Kingmaker', one of the most powerful landowners of the fifteenth century, and died, half-insane, as York's son marched triumphantly into London, in 1471.

of English and Welsh longbowmen. The remorseless forward movement of the French horde presented the English with a wall of bewildered men to cut down. Some of the nobles who had taken bets the night before on who would capture Henry were imprisoned in England. Those of lesser rank were butchered to stop any attempt to attack the isolated English force again.

Later campaigns showed Henry to be a strategist without peer. In one siege he fought in underground saps dug against a city wall, and in another he designed a floating tower with a drawbridge on top. Nobody knows what disease destroyed him at the age thirty-four, only that he spent his last days calmly arranging for the succession of a baby son he had never seen.

Henry V receiving a copy of Thomas Occleve's 'De Regimine Principum' from the author
A manuscript illumination to Occleve's book, and one of the best and most vivid likenesses of Henry. He is shown clean-shaven, with his familiar pudding-bowl hairstyle, dressed in a long fashionable gown. Kings are frequently represented in manuscript illuminations as the recipients of books, often those which they themselves had commissioned.

Henry VI *by an unknown artist*
From a standard portrait of Henry produced by Tudor artists for sets of early kings and queens. These appear to go back to lost pictures from life. The portrait of Henry can be dated on costume to *c.* 1450, and it conforms to a portrait formula evolved by Roger van der Weyden in Flanders. Henry wears a collar of S's, a Lancastrian badge, whose origins are still obscure.

Edward IV

Richard III

Born 1442, reigned 1461–1470 and 1471–1483

Edward III had several children: Richard II was the son of the first, while Henry IV who deposed him was the child of another. Yet another, born in between, was the ancestor of the Duke of York whose son became Edward IV in the fifteenth century. That was the basis of the bloody struggle later described as the Wars of the Roses.

Edward was utterly different from Henry VI, the pious and indecisive king he brushed aside. He was harsh and vigorous, as a victorious commander in those violent times had to be, but he also had a carefree and debonair side. He was unusually tall and good-looking and his delight in attractive women, irrespective of the risk they might bring, cost Edward the support of Warwick the 'Kingmaker',

his most powerful ally. While Warwick was in France on a solemn embassy to win a princess fit to be England's queen, Edward married a pretty young widow from a low stratum of the aristocracy at home.

Warwick, the champion of the house of York, now switched allegiance to Lancaster, deposed Edward and restored Henry VI to the throne. But the Lancastrian triumph was short-lived. At Barnet, less than a year later, the great earl was defeated and killed, and some of his allies condemned. One of these allies was Clarence, a brother of the king, who pardoned him, only to be rewarded by further treachery. Clarence was judicially murdered.

Edward grew fat and died of gluttony, upbraiding his supporters for not saving his brother from his anger.

Born 1452, reigned 1483–1485

Opinion about this king has oscillated between two extremes. One is represented by the Richard of Shakespeare, a monster warped in mind and body, whose unquenchable ambition made him liquidate all who stood between him and the throne. The other extreme is a reaction to that portrait, and its champions find Richard innocent of almost everything of which he was accused. But it is hard to absolve him of the charge of supplanting Edward V, son of his brother Edward IV. The young Edward and his brother were the Princes in the Tower, and although it is not certain that Richard had them killed after he put them there, it is clear that he wanted them out of the way.

Contemporary paintings do not show the hump back which later propaganda gave Richard, and he had many loyal supporters, especially in the north of England. He was a resourceful commander and in some ways a conscientious ruler, and he promoted important legal reforms. But his claim to the crown was flimsy and the early death of his son encouraged opposition. He was defeated and killed at the Battle of Bosworth by a force of what Shakespeare's Richard dismissed as 'a scum of lackey Bretons' who were led by his successor, Henry Tudor.

Edward IV receiving a book from Lord Rivers
A manuscript illumination to the 'Dictes des Philosophes', a translation from the French by Lord Rivers, printed by Caxton, and here turned back into manuscript. Edward IV is shown with his queen, Elizabeth Woodville, his eldest son, the future Edward V (one of the very few representations of him), and behind, Richard of Gloucester (also in ermine robes). Lord Rivers, the queen's brother, was executed by Richard in 1483.

Richard III   *by an unknown artist*
From a late sixteenth-century set of early kings and queens. This is the only conventional portrait type of Richard recorded.

Henry VII

Born 1457, reigned 1485–1509

Sweeping claims have been made about the importance of Henry VII in British history. Some have spoken as if his accession marked the end of the Middle Ages and the birth of modern society and government. Others have implied that he ended civil war by marrying the chief heiress of the rival dynasty. But there is no reason to believe that Henry saw himself as a dramatic innovator. He must sometimes have wondered if he would survive. At the Battle of Bosworth Richard III saw some of his supporters falter, others defect and one of his most loyal lords die early in the conflict. Rather than wait for his army to disintegrate Richard decided to strike directly at Henry. It must have been a chilling moment for the pretender, a Welshman who knew France better than England.

When Henry Tudor invaded England there were no direct descendants of the Lancastrian kings left to claim the throne from York. Henry was the next in line, since his grandfather had married the French widow of Henry V after entering the service of her royal husband as a page. Henry's mother, who had been a widow of fourteen when he was born, claimed descent from Edward III. Such nice legal considerations must have been remote from Henry's mind as Richard galloped straight for him and cut down his standard-bearer. Even as Richard squirmed under the blows of his rival's bodyguard, shouting 'Treason' as he died, Henry must have known that his title would be disputed. The first claimant was crowned in Dublin, but defeated in England. The second said that he was the younger of the Princes in the Tower and was welcomed as such in Scotland, but he failed to topple Henry.

One of the most treasured legacies of the European Renaissance is the work of professional painters quite unlike the monkish illustrators of earlier tradition. The powerful royal portraits produced all over Europe in Tudor times are made all the more convincing by showing clear family traits through the generations. Henry VII has been recorded for us with the rather uncompromising and thin-lipped look that appears time and time again in pictures of his descendants. He was tall, with thin hair and rather poor teeth, and was restrained, calculating and cautious.

Henry VII *by Michiel Sittow*
This small vivid portrait of a shrewd and able man, founder of the Tudor dynasty, brings to English portraiture a wholly new directness and individuality, and is the earliest documented painting from life of an English king. It was painted in 1505 by 'Master Michiel', and sent to a proposed bride for Henry – Margaret, daughter of the Emperor Maximilian. The marriage did not take place.

Henry said in France that as soon as he became King of England he would link York and Lancaster by marrying a niece of Richard III. He stuck to that pledge and married Elizabeth of York, even though it was two years before he saw her.

Explorers who looked for a trade route to Asia across the Atlantic were encouraged in his reign, while over-mighty and ostentatious earls, not to mention priests who kept concubines, were censured. Henry's seizure of power had been encouraged by the early death of the son of Richard III. Henry was shattered when his own elder son died unexpectedly in healthy youth after being carefully matched with a Spanish princess. But another son survived and Henry VII died in peace after a period of government that did not dazzle, but left the Crown richer than it had been for generations.

Henry VII *by Pietro Torrigiana*
A handsome polychrome bust by the Florentine sculptor Torrigiano, probably done from life about 1508–09, shortly before Henry died. Not long afterwards, Torrigiano was to work on the tombs in Westminster Abbey of Henry VII, his wife, Elizabeth of York, and his mother, Lady Margaret Beaufort, who died a few months after her son.

Elizabeth of York *by an unknown artist*
There is only one painted portrait type of Elizabeth, dating from the last years of her life, and this version is probably late sixteenth-century. She holds a white rose, emblem of the house of York, and a reminder of the political and dynastic importance of her marriage, which united the houses of Lancaster and York, bringing peace after the Wars of the Roses. Henry, in Michiel Sittow's portrait, holds a red rose.

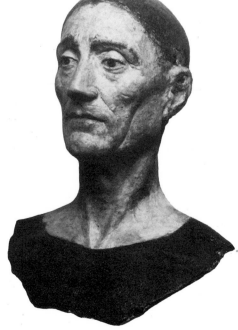

Henry VII *plaster effigy in Westminster Abbey*
Probably taken from a death mask, the stark and strangely compelling face of Henry's funeral effigy provides a remarkable sculptural image. These effigies, probably intended to be recognisable likenesses, were displayed at royal funerals and served the basic political function of showing that the king was indeed dead. The tomb effigy was a later, lasting image. Torrigiano almost certainly used this funeral effigy when working on the bronze figure for Henry's tomb in the Abbey.

21

Henry VIII

Born 1491, reigned 1509–1547

Thanks to the superb painting of Holbein, the appearance of Henry VIII is better known than that of almost any other English sovereign before the invention of photography. The broad, sumptuously arrayed frame with legs planted firmly apart and hands defiantly on hips, the large bearded face topped by a rakish feathered cap; those are the hallmarks that have made this king instantly recognisable to millions through the centuries. But it was only one aspect of the king that Holbein captured so eloquently. Illness and disappointment later reduced Henry to a fat, helpless lump of flesh and foul temper. As a prince and a young king, though, he was brilliant and captivating. At the age of ten he impressed the court by dancing joyously at the wedding of his elder brother to Catherine of Aragon. As a young man he was a tireless and jovial athlete, skilful in music and balladry and with a splendidly bold and handsome air about him.

But whether dancing and jousting in energetic youth or glowering in unsteady middle age Henry was always dangerous. One of his first acts as king was to seek popularity by sentencing two of his father's most strict and efficient advisers to death. His wives knew Henry as a sometimes callous husband, his children often as a heartless father. Many people today who know that Henry had six wives do not know why. He was a womanizer, certainly, but that was not the only motive that made him unceremoniously exchange one spouse for another. He wanted to secure his dynasty by bequeathing the crown to a strong and mature son. Earlier English history provided him with plenty of dismal instances of monarchs who had failed to do that, the most recent example being Richard III who had been destroyed by Henry's own father. But the quest for an heir led Henry into a course that was far more significant for posterity than his six weddings.

His first wife was Catherine of Aragon, his brother's Spanish widow, and special permission had to be won from the Pope before they could marry. When Catherine failed to produce a boy, Henry decided to divorce her, but the Vatican would not allow it. By that time England had felt the reforming zeal of Protestant Europe and an intense religious debate

Henry VIII and Henry VII
by Hans Holbein the Younger
Holbein's cartoon for his great wall painting in the Privy Chamber of Whitehall Palace, finished in 1537 and destroyed by fire in 1698. It was a working drawing, and bears the pinpricks used to transfer the design to the wall. The complete painting included Elizabeth of York and Jane Seymour. The image of Henry is closely connected with the portrait in the Thyssen-Bornemisza Collection.

Henry VIII   *by Hans Holbein the Younger*
Painted about 1536, this is the only surviving painting of Henry which is definitely by Holbein (the Court Painter), and from the life. It is one of the great masterpieces of British portraiture. Sadly, no satisfactory portraits are known of the young Henry, whose handsome looks and athletic prowess were praised by his contemporaries.

Henry VIII   *by an unknown artist*
A copy, probably early seventeenth-century, of the last portrait type of Henry, dating from *c.* 1542. The image is a formidable one, the bulk and splendour of the figure and the ruthless gimlet eyes conveying the power and majesty of the king.

Henry VIII   *by an unknown artist*
Holbein's name tends to be associated indiscriminately with most portraits of Henry VIII, but this is a version of a non-Holbein likeness, produced during the later years of the reign.

23

Catherine of Aragon
attributed to Lucas Hornebolte
An interesting miniature of the first of Henry's six wives. Staunchly Catholic, mother of Mary I but of no surviving son, Catherine was a victim of Henry's political and religious ambitions. She died in 1536 and was buried in Peterborough Abbey.

Jane Seymour   *photogravure of the painting by Hans Holbein the Younger in the Kunsthistorisches Museum, Vienna*
Jane married Henry in 1536, and this portrait was probably painted not long afterwards. She had been lady in waiting to both Catherine of Aragon and Anne Boleyn. Though successful in giving Henry the son he so much wanted (later Edward VI), Jane died soon after his birth. She was only eighteen.

Anne of Cleves   *by Hans Holbein the Younger*
The king's fourth marriage, intended to strengthen England's ties with Protestant Europe, took place in 1539, the year this portrait was painted. It was not a success, and after only six months Henry divorced Anne, who retired to Richmond until her death in 1557.

No authentic likeness is known of Catherine Howard, whose two-year marriage to Henry ended in 1542 with her execution.

Anne Boleyn   *by an unknown artist*
Contemporary accounts of Anne's appearance vary from the hostile to the partisan, agreeing only as to her dark colouring. None of the descriptions accords very closely with the standard surviving portrait type, of which this is an example. Anne wears a B-shaped gold pendant.

had arisen in the country. In this climate Henry pursued his dynastic end by first trying to show that the permission given for him to marry Catherine had been unjustified. The festering dispute with Rome led Henry to take the momentous step of calling himself 'Supreme Head of the Church in England', thus ending centuries of allegiance to Rome in matters of the spirit.

The king married Anne Boleyn, his second wife, in secret in 1533, but she was disposed of three years later on false charges, after failing to produce a son. Jane Seymour, whom Henry married less than a month after Anne's execution, died after giving birth to the long-awaited son, later to be crowned as Edward VI. The next wife, Anne of Cleves, repelled Henry, the one after that, Catherine Howard, deceived him and lost her head for it, and the sixth, Catherine Parr, outlived him.

Many able men were condemned by Henry, including Cardinal Wolsey who virtually governed England for the first twenty years of the reign, Sir Thomas More who rejected the break with Rome, and Thomas Cromwell who engineered the dissolution of the monasteries.

By the time of his death Henry had become about as unpopular as any of the most hated of the rulers of England.

Catherine Parr   *attributed to William Scrots*
This portrait, dating from *c.* 1545, has an uninterrupted history as depicting Catherine from before 1643, and appears to be the only known authentic likeness of Henry's sixth wife. Catherine proved a kind stepmother to Prince Edward and the Princesses Elizabeth and Mary, and she outlived her husband by about a year.

Edward VI

Born 1537, reigned 1547–1553

The son for whom Henry VIII had yearned was an intelligent and independent boy who had time, in a short reign, to give evidence of some of his father's harshness and indifference to suffering. Stories of his enthusiastic skill in classical studies and religious debate would be hard to credit had we not the evidence of some of Edward's exercise books. Three survive, crammed with Cicero and Aristotle, while those of his journals which remain to us include letters and speeches in French, Greek and Latin. It is clear that the boy king was exceptionally precocious and conscious of his royal office. He was a staunch Protestant with a studious teenager's eagerness to join in adult discussion that drew flocks of clucking reformers to his court.

Edward was short, but carried himself with princely bearing. His eyes were rather weak and he soon fell a prey to a succession of diseases. In his fifteenth year he had measles and smallpox and then developed a cough which he could not shake off. He died immediately after repeating a prayer of his own composition and ten years after one of the leading astrologers of Europe had predicted that he would live to middle age.

Edward VI *by an unknown artist*
An anti-papal allegory, painted *c.* 1548–49 to commemorate the renewal of the English Reformation under Edward VI. Henry VIII, on his deathbed, indicates his successor, Edward. On the right stands Protector Somerset, and next to him sit the Duke of Northumberland and Archbishop Thomas Cranmer. With the Bible open at his feet, Edward vanquishes the impurities of the Pope, and inset in the background is a scene of image breaking.

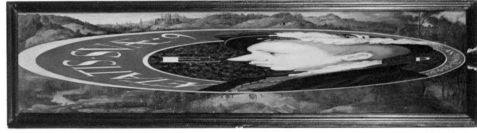

Edward VI *by William Scrots*
The distorted perspective painting (anamorphosis), which falls into place only when seen from the side, seems to have been something of a popular curiosity in the sixteenth century, and this portrait was a showpiece at Whitehall Palace. It is by William Scrots, who succeeded Holbein as King's Painter in 1543, and dates from 1546, the year before Edward succeeded to the throne at the age of nine.

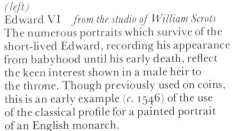

(left)
Edward VI *from the studio of William Scrots*
The numerous portraits which survive of the short-lived Edward, recording his appearance from babyhood until his early death, reflect the keen interest shown in a male heir to the throne. Though previously used on coins, this is an early example (*c.* 1546) of the use of the classical profile for a painted portrait of an English monarch.

Mary 1

Born 1516, reigned 1553–1558

Mary was the first child of Henry VIII, but he wanted neither her nor her mother, Catherine of Aragon. They were sent away from court, and at one time Mary was declared illegitimate. She grew up a staunch Catholic, like her mother, and when Edward VI died in 1553 his most ambitious noble, John Dudley, Duke of Northumberland, tried to exclude Mary by rushing the young Protestant Lady Jane Grey onto the throne. But Mary was too quick for the Protestant faction and was welcomed with joy, for she was patriotic, dedicated, devout and mature. Yet her subjects quickly came to hate their queen for the determination and method with which she tried to reimpose the Roman Catholic faith on England. She concluded a strategically dangerous marriage with the Catholic King Philip II of Spain and earned the nickname 'Bloody Mary' when Cranmer, Archbishop of Canterbury, and other leading churchmen were burned at the stake in her name.

One of the most tragic of English sovereigns, Mary grew up in sorrow and reigned in ardent but desolate conviction. She loved children but had none, and her husband had little taste for England. He left the country after little more than a year.

Mary I and Philip II of Spain
by Jacopo da Trezzo
Two of a number of medals executed by the Italian medallist Jacopo da Trezzo while in the Low Countries, 1555–59. The reverse of the medal of Mary bears a design representing Peace burning the weapons of war and releasing the blind from darkness. Philip was in England only from 1554 to 1555, and again, fleetingly, in 1557. This medal of him is dated 1555.

Mary I *by Hans Eworth*
Hans Eworth, a Netherlandish artist, and Mary's official portraitist, painted this small panel—scarcely more than a large miniature in size—in 1554, soon after her accession. The queen wears the large pendant pearl, 'La Peregrina', traditionally sent to her in June 1554 by Philip II of Spain, whom she married a month later at Winchester.

Mary I *by Master John*
Payment for a painting by Master John, presumably this one, is recorded in the Privy Purse expenses of the Lady Mary in 1544. One of the very few portraits of Mary as princess, it remained in the Brocas family, descendants of Mary's Master of the Buckhounds, until its purchase by the National Portrait Gallery in 1876.

Elizabeth 1

Born 1533, reigned 1558–1603

Elizabeth was the daughter of Anne Boleyn, second wife of Henry VIII. Astrologers had predicted that Elizabeth would be the king's long-awaited son, and Henry was so bitter about the birth of another girl that he did not attend Elizabeth's baptism. He preferred the baby Elizabeth to his other daughter Mary, however, until Anne fell from favour and was executed. Then Elizabeth was declared a bastard. When Mary was queen she tried to force an unwilling Elizabeth to attend mass and imprisoned her on suspicion of encouraging a Protestant revolt. Those dangerous years turned the young princess into an expert diplomat and at the same time a waverer who dithered before reaching decisions. They also made the childless Elizabeth reluctant to name an heir while she was queen. She did not want anyone to play the part with her that she had played with Mary.

It was an inauspicious beginning, and when Elizabeth succeeded Mary at the age of twenty-five she faced a morose and divided country. The new queen was striking and red-haired, and her appearance is well known to us through countless paintings that show a small, rather

Elizabeth I *by Nicholas Hilliard*
Dated 1572, this candid and convincing likeness is the earliest of several miniatures of Elizabeth by Nicholas Hilliard, her court goldsmith, carver and limner. The son of a goldsmith, and trained as one himself, Hilliard produced portrait miniatures of meticulously fine and jewel-like quality. Portraits 'in little', a particularly personal art form, were popular and fashionable in Elizabethan England; they were intended to be held in the hand or worn close to the heart—or even on hats or shoe buckles.

serious face with thin Tudor lips peering from the top of a monstrous pile of drapes and jewels. She was good at languages, well read and she appreciated the theatre. She enjoyed wit and delighted in dancing and joking with her courtiers. But if anyone went too far the laughing countenance froze and the regal Tudor upholder of sovereignty took over. Elizabeth proved in maturity that England had for once found a monarch who fully matched and complemented her age. She was dazzling, energetic, daring and increasingly powerful—and so was Elizabethan England. Shakespeare, Spenser, Marlowe, Tallis and Hilliard were among the brilliant artists of her reign while Drake and Hawkins were among the adventurers who harried England's overbearing rival, Spain, with the support of England's queen.

We know a lot about Elizabeth and have much first-hand evidence on which to work. A good deal of her writing has survived including the characteristic bold signature with its elaborate curls and squiggles that is reproduced on modern pound notes. Yet Elizabeth I remains mysterious. Some have even suggested that she was a man. She baffled contemporaries, too, dangling many suitors on long and painful strings and resisting all attempts to manoeuvre her into a safe

Elizabeth I *by an unknown artist*
Elizabeth was well aware of the importance of the state portrait, and had strong views on how she should be portrayed. Strenuous efforts were made to confine portraits of her to those derived from a few authorised 'face masks' or patterns, an attempt to reconcile the reality of a great but ageing woman with the cult of Gloriana, the Virgin Queen, symbol of Church and State. This is one of the finest portraits of Elizabeth, but already (*c.* 1575) the face is becoming a formalised mask of majesty.

(lower right) **Elizabeth I**
attributed to Robert Peake the Elder
Though known as the 'Procession to Blackfriars', the occasion represented here is uncertain. Probably a procession of this kind was customary when Elizabeth went out and about during the later years of her reign. She is attended by her courtiers and ladies and by several Garter Knights. The stiff and splendid figure of the queen somehow suggests a religious as well as a royal progress, and the picture conveys something of the extraordinary loyalty and devotion she inspired.

POSVI DEVM ADIVTOREM MEVM

SEMPER EADEM.

Elizabeth I *by Crispin van de Passe the Elder after Isaac Oliver*
This wonderfully elaborate engraving probably commemorates the death of the queen, which is referred to in the inscription. The background was added by the engraver, who shows Elizabeth with orb and sceptre, Bible and sword beside her. She is magnificently attired, and wears the flat-topped farthingale fashionable at the end of the reign.

Elizabeth I *by Steven van Herwijck*
Though somewhat corroded – it was unearthed during ploughing at Great Moulton, Norfolk, in 1962 – this is a fine medallic portrait of Elizabeth. It is of lead (4·8 cm (1⅞ in) diameter), and dates from 1565, one of several portrait medals by Steven van Herwijck, who visited England in the 1560s. The reverse shows Faith clasping a cross.

Elizabeth I *by an unknown sculptor*
Possibly one of the 'foure livelie statues all wrought in white marble' of the four later Tudor monarchs, recorded in 1590 in the inventory of Lumley Castle, seat of the Earls of Scarborough. It is one of the few known busts of Elizabeth, and appears to be based on the medal of her by Steven van Herwijck.

(right) **Elizabeth I** *by or after George Gower*
A version of the new portrait pattern of Elizabeth which came into circulation soon after 1588 and commemorates the defeat that year of the Spanish Armada. Probably by George Gower, Serjeant Painter to the Queen from 1581, this painting has been cut down on all sides and retains only a glimpse of the naval battle scenes which appear in the background of other versions of the picture, such as the one at Woburn Abbey.

dynastic marriage that would promise a strong succession. Her main rivals were the leaders of two Catholic powers. Scotland frightened her because when dominated by French influence it enabled France to 'bestride the realm' of England. Mary, Queen of Scots, who was descended from a sister of Henry VIII, claimed to be Queen of England, too. She was executed in 1587 after incautiously encouraging a wild plot against Elizabeth. Mary had already spent nineteen years in English captivity.

Elizabeth's deadliest rival, however, was the king of Spain, Philip II, widower of her predecessor on the English throne.

Raids on his overseas empire by daring Englishmen goaded him into open war, and in 1588 he launched his great Armada of fighting ships against England. It was attacked and scattered in the English Channel by Lord Howard of Effingham and Sir Francis Drake, and driven up the North Sea. The danger from Spain was removed, and Elizabeth went on to become one of the best-loved sovereigns of English history.

Elizabeth never lost her imperiousness. On her deathbed, when told by her secretary of state that she should rest, she spat at him 'Little man, the word *must* is not used with princes.'

James 1

Born 1566, reigned 1603–1625

Elizabeth I, one of the most English of sovereigns, travelled widely in her kingdom but never left it. When she died childless the best claimant to succeed her was a Scotsman. To add to the irony, James VI of Scotland was the son of Mary, Queen of Scots, who had once set her sights on the English throne and had been put to death for plotting to seize it. As king of Scotland James showed some firmness with his turbulent subjects, but as king of both countries he combined dangerous obstinacy with fatal partiality and indecision. Succeeding Elizabeth when he was thirty-seven, he thought that his experience in Scotland had turned him into a skilful ruler. He clung to the inflexible doctrine that monarchs ruled by Divine Right, and had many clashes with restive parliaments.

James's character was complex; he could be both refined and coarse, resolute and wavering, slovenly and regal. He was tall, broad-shouldered with rather spindly legs, unattractive to look at and

Anne of Denmark *by Isaac Oliver*
Oliver was the queen's official miniaturist, and this is one of his most beautiful portraits of her. The unusually elaborate costume and hairstyle have led in the past to the mistaken impression that she is in masque costume.

James I *engraving by Simon van de Passe*
One of the plates to the *Bazilologia*, a series of engraved portraits of British monarchs, first published in 1618.

James I *by Daniel Mytens*
A moving portrait of the old king, bowed down by cares of office and his heavy Garter robes, painted in 1621. This was the last official state portrait for which he sat.

hear, but sharply intelligent. He was one of the most uncouth kings of England, with a liking for noisy banquets and raucous scatological jokes. As a Protestant king, he was the target of the Gunpowder Plot hatched in 1605 by Roman Catholic sympathisers, including Guy Fawkes. Yet he indulged delusions of grandeur by concocting schemes for grand European alliances, including one with Roman Catholic Spain, through royal marriages. Dubbed 'the wisest fool in Christendom', one of his greatest weaknesses was indulgence of a succession of male favourites at court. Some have since judged from the evidence of his gushing correspondence with them that he was helplessly bisexual. The king's most notorious attachment was to George Villiers, who was hoisted swiftly through a series of offices and titles to become Duke of Buckingham. They met when the king was forty-seven and the favourite twenty-two and James was infatuated.

Buckingham survived James, but the king proved himself a dangerous and unreliable master to others, among them Sir Walter Raleigh, the Elizabethan buccaneer who offended Spain, who was condemned on a trumped up charge in 1618.

Inept as he was, James I gave evidence of finer qualities by supporting the stupendous project of translation that produced the Authorized Version of the Bible.

Henry, Prince of Wales
by Robert Peake the Elder
A striking full-length by Henry's Court Painter. Henry was immensely talented and cultivated, and his early death (in 1612) from typhoid fever was regarded as a national tragedy.

James I when James VI of Scotland
by an unknown artist (detail)
A relatively recent portrait based on a foreign engraving of c. 1595–1600. James disliked having his portrait painted, which may explain the scarcity of satisfactory likenesses. He is seen here before he became the enfeebled figure shown in the final portrait.

Charles 1

Born 1600, reigned 1625–1649

As a baby Charles was not expected to live, and as a child he was overshadowed by his elder brother, Henry. But the death of that prince made Charles heir to the throne and set him on a romantic and tragic path which led to the executioner's block. He grew up a small, stammering Scotsman with inflexible ideals but without the will to impose them on his subjects or the respect needed to win full support. Charles was an unapproachable, correct and fastidious king who acquired an exceptionally fine collection of paintings for his country and patronized notable artists like Van Dyck. The king was far more successful in private life than in government. Some of the most powerful and uncompromising men in England objected to his concept of monarchy, to his advisers, to his religion and to his queen.

Charles had a strong and sincere belief in the Divine Right of Kings and the corresponding duties of subjects. After early disagreements with Parliament he ruled without it for more than a decade and on the eve of the Civil War in 1642 tried to arrest five MPs who opposed him. Henrietta Maria, the Roman Catholic French princess whom Charles married, came to England with a full entourage and aroused persistent resentment among her husband's Protestant subjects. In

Charles I *by Daniel Mytens*
A distinguished full-length of Charles dating from 1631. Daniel Mytens, a Dutchman, was the leading court painter before the arrival of Van Dyck in the early 1630s. His solid and elegant portraits marked the advent of a new style.

The five eldest children of Charles I
after Sir Anthony Van Dyck
A copy of the well-known picture of the royal children painted in 1637. Prince Charles, the future Charles II, is shown in the centre, with Princess Mary, the Princess Royal, and James, Duke of York, later James II, on the left, and Princess Elizabeth and Princess Anne on the right. Van Dyck conveys the engaging charm of the children while at the same time satisfying the demands of formal state portraiture.

matters religious the high Anglicanism adopted by the king, and pursued vigorously by William Laud, his Archbishop of Canterbury, inflamed Puritan feeling. Politics were soured further by clear evidence that the king, for all his high-minded philosophy, was deceitful and weak. On the eve of his execution Charles paused to regret being pushed into signing the death warrant of his ablest administrator, Strafford, eight years earlier. He attacked powerful men through their purses by levying special taxes to pay for shipbuilding. Earlier rulers had raised the money on the coast, but Charles demanded it inland as well.

It was more than fifteen years before the mixture of grievance and determination boiled into civil war. Feelings about who was right in that conflict remain lively and some modern supporters of each side dress up as flamboyant Cavaliers and dour Roundheads to re-enact the battles. The war went well for Charles at first, but he lost London early and set up his headquarters in Oxford. The university city was loyal, but London was richer and more resilient. The impact of Oliver Cromwell and his force of Ironsides was decisive and in 1645 the king abandoned the armed struggle for his realm. After two years of lonely and ignominious efforts to win support and to compromise with his enemies Charles was brought to trial. He refused to recognise the court but was sentenced nevertheless. He said: 'Death is not terrible to me' and went calmly to the block.

Charles was at his most impressive in defeat, while his enemies were gross and vindictive in their triumph. Just as the Queen today is said to guarantee constitutional stability by being outside politics, so Charles has been portrayed as a guardian of popular liberty against a narrow clique. Others have seen him as a devious and unimaginative tyrant. The debate is not over yet.

Henrietta Maria   *after Sir Anthony Van Dyck*
A copy of one of Van Dyck's most tender and beautiful portraits of the queen. The original was painted around 1636, and the attitude of the arms suggests that Henrietta is pregnant, perhaps carrying Princess Anne (born 1637).

Charles I   *by Gerard Honthorst*
A vivid and engaging study of the young king, who looks up suddenly as if disturbed while reading a book. Honthorst came to England in 1628 and painted a large allegory of Mercury presenting the Arts to Apollo and Diana in the persons of Charles I and Henrietta Maria. This study relates to the figure of Charles as Apollo.

Charles I with Sir Edward Walker
by an unknown artist
This picture was probably commissioned by Walker, who was Garter-King-at-Arms, and shows an incident during the Civil War, perhaps one of the engagements in the West Country campaigns of 1644–45. The portrait is not contemporary; the figure of Charles is based on Lely's portrait of 1647.

(right) Charles I   *by Sir Anthony Van Dyck*
One of the noblest and most heroic of all British royal portraits, dating from around 1637–38. A tablet on the tree bears the inscription, 'CAROLUS/REX MAGNAE/BRITANIAE' (Charles, King of Great Britain). The equestrian portrait has possessed connotations of imperialism and military glory since classical times, and Van Dyck interprets the sensitive character of Charles through this tradition. The portrait belongs to a great sequence of royal commissions in which Van Dyck established the dominant types of state portrait for the next century or more.

Charles II

Born 1630, reigned 1660–1685

Whatever else may be said of the patron of Nell Gwyn and the Royal Society, he was never dull. Charles is said to have begun a busy love-life at the age of fifteen with a former governess. His subsequent career has a strong appeal to the modern fashion for self-deprecation, non-violence and wry humour. It is a dangerous appeal because it makes Charles look too much like a twentieth-century playboy rather than a seventeenth-century head of state with power of life and death over his subjects. But the pitfalls of historical interpretation do not detract from the story of the man's life. The anecdote about his hiding in an oak tree while Cromwell's soldiers beat the bushes underneath is well known. Soon after that incident he travelled in the disguise of a woman's servant reading his 'wanted' posters and chatting with earnest anti-royalists about his own disgraceful behaviour. Devoted supporters helped Charles to escape to France whence Cromwell's spies sent back reports about 'fornication, drunkenness and adultery' in the pretender's court of exiles.

The restoration of the monarchy in 1660 was greeted with joy in England and Charles showed himself to be an exceptionally affable king, tall, merry, energetic, with a love of hawking, riding and feasting. Paintings show an appropriately sensual face, occasionally with a neat toothbrush moustache that emphasises the pleasure-seeking image. His marriage to a Roman Catholic princess from Portugal, Catherine of Braganza, who did not speak English, did not persuade him to abandon mistresses. He enjoyed them, gave them titles and acknowledged thirteen illegitimate children. One especially attractive girl repulsed him so firmly that courtiers took bets on the outcome of the pursuit. The king wrote a poem about it which included the refrain: 'I think there's no hell like loving too well'.

Nell Gwyn, the actress who had once sold oranges in the theatre, called the King 'Charles III' because she had already had two lovers of the same name. Charles had a happy relationship of deep understanding with her which contrasts strongly with life inside the royal family. He bustled his niece into a political marriage with the Prince of Orange when she was an unwilling fifteen-year-old.

Charles II *by Honoré Pelle*
This magnificent bust by a French sculptor has a sense of movement and vitality rare in British sculpture. The elaborate detail is superbly realized, and it sets off the witty and sardonic character of the king. The bust is dated 1684, and another slightly earlier version is known.

Charles II when Prince of Wales
after Adriaen Hanneman
A version of a portrait of the young Charles in armour, painted when he was in exile in Holland around 1648. He wears the ribbon of the Garter. The original painting has not been traced, but several versions exist, some of them threequarter-length. Charles was painted by other Dutch and Flemish artists during his years of exile, but though engravings of these portraits exist, originals and painted copies are rare.

Charles was much amused at the sight of the unsmiling Dutchman approaching the bedroom on his wedding night.

The foreign policy of Charles II is often regarded as a shambles of dilatory and shifting diplomacy in which Protestant Dutchmen raided the Medway towns while the Roman Catholic king of France paid cash for English concessions. Like his grandfather, James I, Charles was more extravagant than the revenues of the Crown would allow. One of his economy measures was to restrict ten-course dinners in the court to himself, the queen, his brother and his sister-in-law.

Charles was an enthusiastic amateur scientist and a devoted theatre-goer. Newton and Hooke, prominent in the development, respectively, of the telescope and microscope, worked in his reign. So did Dryden, Wren, Pepys and Purcell. Later Englishmen looked back fondly to 'Good King Charles's golden days'.

This king, who retained his humour to the end, said on his deathbed: 'I am sorry, gentlemen, for being so unconscionable a time a'dying'.

Charles II *by Samuel Cooper*
A large and splendid miniature of Charles in Garter robes, dated 1665. Cooper had been appointed limner to the king soon after the Restoration, and he painted some of his greatest works for his royal patron.

Born 1633, reigned 1685–1688

Like George VI, father of the present Queen, James held the title of Duke of York as the second son of a reigning monarch. Again like George VI, he succeeded his elder brother as king. Unfortunately for James–and for England–he lacked the ability of Charles II to dissemble about his religion. Less than ten years after the Restoration James was hearing mass every day in London. His second wife was an Italian princess who was said by some excited English Protestants to be a daughter of the Pope. James liked other men's wives as much as Charles had, but he lacked his brother's humour. Nell Gwyn called James 'Dismal Jimmy', and there is no record that he ever told or enjoyed a joke. He lived in an age of acute religious sensitivity and it needed a more imaginative touch than his to survive it.

James's main rival was the Duke of Monmouth, a Protestant illegitimate son of Charles II, who invaded England in 1685 and was defeated at the Battle of Sedgemoor. This was the last battle fought upon English soil. Monmouth was taken and executed, and his supporters were condemned by the hundred in the 'Bloody Assize' of Judge Jeffreys.

James's high-handed imposition of Roman Catholicism on England became

Catherine of Braganza *by or after Dirk Stoop*
A version of a portrait painted in Portugal shortly before Catherine's marriage to Charles II in 1662. She is dressed in the Portuguese fashion, in a wide hooped skirt, which caused some amusement in court circles when she first arrived in England.

Charles II *attributed to Thomas Hawker*
A late portrait of Charles in which the florid conventions of Restoration art are given full rein. The lavish accessories are matched by a swirling, sensuous design that emphasises the pleasure-loving character of the king. Hawker, an obscure artist, had been a pupil of Sir Peter Lely.

James II when Duke of York
by Samuel Cooper
James, who was a considerable patron of the arts, sat to Cooper, the greatest English portraitist of the age, on several occasions. This miniature, dated 1661, is the earliest of those recorded.

James II *by Sir Godfrey Kneller*
A distinguished full-length of James by the leading court painter of the period. It originally depicted him as Lord High Admiral, shortly before his accession in 1684, with his flagship firing a broadside in the background. The regalia was added subsequently to bring the portrait up to date when he became king.

James II *engraving by John Smith after Nicolas de Largillière*
Largillière, a French artist, had to leave England at the time of the Test Act which penalized Catholics. Asked to return by James II, he painted a strikingly elegant portrait of his new patron. He later worked for the Jacobite court in exile.

increasingly resented until William of Orange, husband of James's daughter Mary, was asked to invade as a champion of Protestantism with a claim to the throne. The king fled, failed to recapture his kingdom, and died in France after more than a decade in exile.

William III when Prince of Orange *by Jan de Baen*
Painted in Holland when William was eighteen. He is dressed as Mercury for a masque held at the Hague in February 1668 to celebrate the Peace of Breda, and this explains the fanciful nature of the portrait. According to a contemporary source, William appeared 'after the Roman fashion, very richly dressed, and with a flourishing hat and feathers'.

James II when Duke of York with his first wife, Anne Hyde *by Sir Peter Lely*
An excellent example of the double portrait format developed by Lely, dating from the mid 1660s. The sitters, dressed in sumptuous costumes, are flanked by billowing curtains, with an Arcadian landscape setting behind.

James holds the baton of a commander while his wife rests his helmet on her lap. Lely, the leading court painter of the Restoration, painted a great series of portraits of naval commanders for James, as well as the famous set of the 'Windsor Beauties'.

William III when Prince of Orange *after Sir Peter Lely*
A version of a popular portrait of William, apparently painted on his visit to England in 1677 to marry Mary. He is represented as a commander, wearing armour and holding a baton, while a battle takes place in the background. He had recently successfully defended the Netherlands against an Anglo-French alliance.

William III & Mary II

Mary II *silver medallion*
Executed in Holland around 1690 by an
unknown artist.

William III Born 1650, reigned
1688–1702
Mary II Born 1662, reigned 1688–1694

Like his namesake, the Conqueror, William III led a successful invasion of England with an army. But unlike the earlier king he did not seize the crown by destroying the reigning monarch in battle. That was not at all what he wanted; indeed there is evidence that he did not even want to depose James II, but merely to halt that king's policy of returning England to Roman Catholicism. William's title was Prince of Orange and its holder was an intensely patriotic Dutch Protestant whose main aim in adult life was to prevent an aggressive and expansionist Roman Catholic France from engulfing his homeland. England under Charles II had been a notoriously unreliable ally, while under James II it was a potential enemy. Yet William did not have to seize power in England. It was handed to him by Protestants who asked him to invade and by James who fled to France without a fight.

James's ignominious exit left England and Scotland with a king who knew little of either and did not grow to love them. William was small, pale, self-contained and never fully mastered colloquial English. His mother was a daughter of Charles I of England and his father a Dutch prince. This gave him a tenuous claim to the English throne, and William strengthened it enormously by marrying a daughter of James II. That match gave his assumption of power in England a valuable tinge of respectability. The marriage was political, and Mary, the young bride, wept before and during the ceremony; she was fifteen while William, at twenty-seven, was four inches shorter than her, slightly hunched and humourless. Charles II thought the arrangement a huge joke. But the couple found a deep and enduring affection so that when Mary died of smallpox at the age of thirty-two the king was distracted with grief. In a lifetime of struggle with France he had known little friendship and less love and his Mary was irreplaceable. She in turn had come to love Holland much more than England and to be haunted by remorse about the fate of her father, who outlived her.

William was convinced that the Dutch people were too disunited to defy the power of Louis XIV of France, the most powerful and dazzling sovereign of his age. Some Dutchmen felt that William was out simply to enlarge his own power. When he invaded England, he sailed under banners that said 'For Religion And Liberty'. But once crowned joint ruler with his wife he found that the English appetite for liberty from the power of the Crown was not to his taste. The sovereign's right to dismiss Parliament, to raise money and to keep a standing army in peacetime, were all curtailed by Parliament in William's reign. He was exasperated.

William is best known in Europe for his stand against France. But in Britain, especially in Ireland, he is remembered as the 'King Billy' who checked the advance of Catholicism by his victory over James at the Battle of the Boyne, in 1690. William fought there not so much for religion as against France, which had promoted the attack by James.

William died as the result of a fall from his horse which had stumbled on a molehill. For some time afterwards, supporters of the exiled members of the Stuart royal family used to drink a toast 'To the little gentleman in black velvet'.

William III and Mary II *engraving by C. Allard after R. de Hooghe*
William and Mary are enthroned, with people bowing to them and a view of Whitehall behind. William holds a globe showing his possessions, with the inscription 'Liberanda Libera', and the royal arms are displayed in the foreground with medallions of earlier kings. The print illustrates a Dutch broadside.

Anne

Born 1665, reigned 1702–1714

Anne, the last of the Stuart monarchs in England, has been given a bad press. She has been portrayed as a dull, objectionable, obstinate and unattractive woman with the peevishness and inability to inspire found in some earlier members of her unhappy dynasty. Her critics say that she was an oasis of mediocrity in a reign of outstanding martial and literary achievement among Englishmen. Her consort, George, Prince of Denmark, who could not speak English really well after twenty years in the country, has been considered the one person at court even less interesting than the queen. But she cannot be assessed fairly if her domestic sufferings are not examined first. The future George I was one of her suitors, but on landing in England he was immediately called back by his father to marry someone else. That slight was nothing compared with Anne's tragedy as a mother.

She became pregnant eighteen times, but only five of her babies were born alive. The longest-lived was the frail little Duke of Gloucester who died at the age of eleven. They were all dead by the time Anne became Queen.

Anne was devoted to the Protestant religion, more so, indeed, than to her father, the Roman Catholic James II. She wondered if her succession of still-

Queen Anne as Princess of Denmark with her son, the Duke of Gloucester
after Sir Godfrey Kneller
The Duke is shown in skirts, so the portrait was probably painted shortly before Easter 1694 when he was breeched. He was the only one of Queen Anne's many children to survive beyond infancy, but was always sickly and died from scarlet fever in 1700 at the age of eleven.

births and puny infants was a punishment for deserting him when William III invaded England. In her reign, some of the greatest British military victories were won by John Churchill, Duke of Marlborough. His palace in Oxfordshire, commissioned by the queen herself, was named after one of them, the Battle of Blenheim (1704). His wife and Anne were close – some would say unhealthily close – friends from childhood well into adult life. She and her sister, Mary II, had the most bitter quarrel of their lives when Marlborough was dismissed from all his offices by William, probably for plotting with the exiled James.

Her domestic life may well have been a troubled one, but her reign witnessed not only the unique military successes of Marlborough but also the Act of Union of 1707 which ended the constitutional separation of England and Scotland. The work of men like Locke, Pope, Swift, Defoe and Vanbrugh (who also designed Blenheim Palace) made the reign as brilliant in English letters as it was squalid in politics. The queen distrusted parties but had to endure a constant struggle for power between Whig and Tory factions. When she lay in her final illness two great lords abused each other passionately over her bed.

Queen Anne   *effigy in Westminster Abbey*
One of a remarkable group of late seventeenth and early eighteenth-century effigies. The early ones, like that of Charles II, were genuine funeral effigies, but the later group were added to supplement the existing collection, which was on view to the public. The head and hands of Anne's effigy are of wax and were modelled, very realistically, sometime in 1714–15. The figure is stuffed and covered with canvas. The robes were not purchased till 1740, but may have been contemporary with Anne. They are one of the most interesting costume survivals of their kind.

Queen Anne   *by David le Marchand*
Le Marchand was an artist of French origin, whose delicate profile portraits in ivory were much admired. This medallion shows his superb craftsmanship and elegance of design at their best.

Queen Anne when Princess   *engraving by A. Blooteling after Sir Peter Lely*
A rare portrait of the queen as a child. The whereabouts of Lely's original oil painting is unknown.

George 1

Born 1660, reigned 1714–1727

This ruler of Hanover who sailed for England in 1714 was a gruff warrior seasoned in many European wars. He spoke several languages but never learned English, and as George I he spent little time in his new kingdom. George was realistic enough to appreciate why he had acquired the throne. It was less that Englishmen wanted him than that they did not want someone else. His attraction was that he was Protestant, while the most direct heir, James Edward, son of the deposed James II, was Roman Catholic. George became king by Act of Parliament rather than by succession, although he could claim descent from James I. His Stuart rival, known as the Old Pretender, tried to win his inheritance by invasion, but failed when French support collapsed. The succession of George I marked a switch from an Anglo-Scottish monarchy to an Anglo-German line which has not been interrupted since.

One of George's first acts in England was to make his favourite mistress a duchess. He had already locked his wife away, after surprising her in a furtive affair with a man whose rapid disappearance has never been explained. George has been judged innocent of the murder purely because he was somewhere else at the time. He kept his wife in a castle until she died more than thirty years later and refused to let their children see her.

George I   *studio of Sir Godfrey Kneller*
Probably produced in Kneller's studio soon after George's arrival in England in 1714, this profile portrait was painted for the coinage. The tradition of using portraits for this purpose can be traced back to Samuel Cooper's profile drawing of Charles II, and later examples include a profile painting by Allan Ramsay of George III.

George I   *by John Michael Rysbrack*
Rysbrack, another foreign artist working in England, and a leading sculptor of the period, produced several busts and statues of George I. This one, in terracotta, shows the king in classical guise, with laurel crown and lion armour. Its date is uncertain, and it may not be from life.

(*left*) George I   *studio of Sir Godfrey Kneller*
A rather crude version of Kneller's coronation portrait of 1714, showing the king in Garter robes. George I's appearance is known to us chiefly through the work of the German artist Kneller, who came to England in 1676, and rapidly established himself as the leading portrait painter. His work as court painter spanned five reigns, and he was responsible for the production of more royal portraits and copies than any artist before or since.

George I   *engraving after John Croker*
Based on the official gold medal struck in 1714 to mark George's coronation, and closely related to the profile painting of the king by Kneller (see above). The king is represented in formal classical style, wearing armour and a laurel wreath. The medal was the work of John Croker, well known engraver and medallist, and chief engraver at the mint.

George II

Born 1683, reigned 1727–1760

The age of the Hanoverian kings in Britain is remembered as one of vivid extremes and contrasts. The rich basked in splendour and the poor swarmed in squalor. Expansion overseas was encouraged by great victories over other European powers in remote lands and politics were enhanced by great statesmen at home. The royal family was notable for remarkably bitter internal quarrels. Before George II became king, he fell out with his father, George I. The old man was jealous of his son's popularity in England, and kept him out of government. When he succeeded, George II quarrelled with his own eldest son. Few British monarchs can have been lampooned more than George II, and scandalous stories were spread about the queen and their chief minister, Sir Robert Walpole.

George combined a love of Britain with a supposedly Germanic liking for detail and precision. He used to visit one mistress at the same time every day, stalking impatiently about his apartments until the clock struck. Under Walpole's ministry there was a strong belief in the country that British interests were being sacrificed to those of Hanover. On one of his European expeditions George II became the last British monarch to lead his troops into battle, at Dettingen in 1743. The elder Pitt said that to foreign eyes Britain had begun to look like the province of a 'despicable' Hanover.

George was a child when the Roman Catholic James II was deposed in England, in 1688. At one moment he thought he might himself be unseated by a descendant of James. This was Prince Charles Edward Stuart, the 'Young Pretender', who landed in Scotland and pushed well into the centre of England. George was ready to pack his bags, but instead of pressing on to London the Pretender retired to Scotland where his force was crushed with appalling cruelty by one of the king's sons, the Duke of Cumberland, at Culloden in 1746. The escape of Bonnie Prince Charlie afterwards has passed into Scottish folklore.

The last of the Stuart claimants to the English throne perished appropriately enough in Rome long after George had died in England. George wanted to be buried next to his dead queen, so that their dust would mingle.

Frederick, Prince of Wales, and his sisters: 'The Music Party' *by Philip Mercier*
A charming painting, dated 1733, of Frederick playing the cello, Anne the harpsichord and Caroline the mandora; Amelia holds a volume of Milton. In the background is the Dutch House at Kew, Anne's home before her marriage. By contrast with his father, George II, Frederick was artistic and cultivated, and a discerning collector of pictures and works of art. He died in 1751 (before his father), aged forty-four. Mercier, a French artist much influenced by Watteau, was his principal painter at this time.

George II *by George, 1st Marquess Townshend*
Townshend's satirical drawings of his contemporaries are among the first genuine caricatures to be produced in this country. He was spirited and witty, and a considerable military and political figure. Though no supporter of the Hanoverians, he treats George II quite mildly, and comparison with other portraits suggests that this is an excellent likeness.

George II *by or after Thomas Worlidge*
This profile portrait emphasises the king's protuberant eyes, prominent nose and receding forehead, features also noted in contemporary comments on his appearance. The painting dates from about 1753, and is unlikely to be from life; George II was a reluctant sitter, and Worlidge a relatively minor artist.

George III

Born 1738, reigned 1760–1820

George III was an uninspiring and inflexible monarch whose exceptionally long reign spanned a period of great brilliance and profound change. He lived to see his kingdom lose its American colonies, and embark upon a period of unprecedented industrial advance. He remained king of England while the king of France was swept away by revolution, and he survived to see his country ride out the threat of domination by Napoleon.

George came to the throne a rather limited young man, with full lips and a large nose. He retained an exacting sense of duty and propriety as long as he was sane, and was to be outraged and wounded by the amorous and financial excesses of his sons. While the aristocracy gloried in wealth and refinement the king believed strongly in plenty of fresh air and a simple diet. He used a prayer book in which all references to the monarch were crossed out and replaced with 'a most miserable sinner'.

Unlike the first two Hanoverian kings of Britain George III was born and educated in this country. He wanted to marry an English girl but was deflected by his mother and married Charlotte,

heiress to a tiny German state unknown to almost everyone in England. The prospective bridegroom was disappointed with his princess, and the English girl he had wanted to marry was a bridesmaid at their wedding. Early in his reign George was derided as the puppet of his mother and a clique of unscrupulous ministers. He tended to be served by men of little merit and sparkle and opposed by brilliant, vain and opportunist rogues.

The main exception came with the rise of the younger Pitt, after George had for once outwitted a government, in this case over a Bill that would have allowed Parliament rather than the Crown to choose the officials who would rule India. Success was cut short by the king's lapse into a mysterious disease, probably of the blood, that reduced him to intermittent derangement for the last twenty years of his life. His condition sometimes made him talk incessantly and hate music, which he normally loved. In his many lucid moments George said he would rather die than go mad. The worst fears of those around him were confirmed by certain incidents: the king once mistook an oak tree for a foreign ambassador, bowed, shook it by a branch and chatted to it about politics. But this did not happen every day. George was goaded by political opponents and mocked by several of his fifteen legitimate children who included his successors George IV and William IV. With the people at large, however, he remained extremely popular. There are numerous testimonies to this, not least those monuments still to be seen up and down England, which were erected to celebrate his recoveries from illness.

George III, Queen Charlotte and their six eldest children *engraving by Richard Earlom after John Zoffany*
The royal family in 1770, wearing the popular Van Dyck costume. Prince Frederick, later Duke of York, stands between his father and Prince George, later George IV; Prince William, later William IV, plays with a cockatoo. George III was a simple homely man, devoted to his family. Queen Charlotte bore him nine sons and six daughters. Zoffany, a German artist, worked mainly in England, where he became well known for his portraits, theatrical scenes and conversation pieces.

George III *studio of Allan Ramsay*
A threequarter-length version of Ramsay's state portrait of the king in coronation robes. This is based on the full-length in the Royal Collection, painted soon after George III's accession in 1760. The countless requests for replicas of this official portrait, and for the companion painting of Queen Charlotte, kept a 'production line' of assistants employed for some twenty years. Ramsay came to London from Edinburgh, and was appointed principal painter to George III.

George III *by F. Hardenberg*
This polychrome plaster statuette (28·6 cm (11¼ in) high) is an unusual and curiously appealing likeness of the king in his later years. He wears the Garter star on his coat, and carries an ear trumpet in his left hand. The figure is posthumous and probably based on a portrait of a few years earlier. On the back of the plinth is inscribed: Published 8 May 1820, by F. Hardenberg 19 Mount St. Grosvenor Sqre. London. George III died in January 1820.

TEMPERANCE enjoying a Frugal Meal.

George IV

Born 1762, reigned 1820–1830

No British monarch combined wit, extravagance, charm and taste to the same degree as George IV. As a young prince he was tall with rather chubby good looks and extravagant in taste and in love. As an old king he was an embarrassing, corpulent voluptuary bursting out of his clothes. He loathed his father and outraged him with foul language and persistent drunkenness. But a far greater offence was his marriage to a Roman Catholic widow, Mrs Fitzherbert. He was later induced to marry a fat, ugly and loud-mouthed Protestant princess whom he disliked from the start. He had to drink himself almost to insensibility before the wedding, but the match was demanded before Parliament would accept responsibility for his colossal debts.

George IV is best remembered as the Prince Regent during his father's final long illness. He established a superb collection of paintings, patronized splendid 'Regency' architecture of lasting excellence and eagerly devoured the works of Jane Austen and Sir Walter Scott. The spendthrift magnificence of his life is best commemorated in the oriental extravaganza of a pavilion which he commis-

George III   *by James Gillray*
The reigns of George III and George IV were the heyday of the satirical caricature, and Gillray was its most brilliant exponent. His output was immense, and many of his caricatures ridicule the habits of the royal family. Here he mocks the supposed miserliness of the king and queen. The print is a companion to his engraving of the Prince of Wales, later George IV, entitled 'A Voluptuary under the Horrors of Digestion'. Both were published in 1792.

George IV   *by James Gillray*
The extravagance and self-indulgence of the Prince of Wales made him an obvious target for cartoonists and satirists. Here, in a companion to his caricature of George III's frugality, Gillray ridicules the Prince's gastronomic excesses. The dice-box in the foreground is an allusion to his gambling habits, and a mock coat of arms hangs on the wall.

A VOLUPTUARY, under the horrors of Digestion.

George IV   *studio of Sir Thomas Lawrence*
A version of the portrait exhibited at the Royal Academy in 1815, the sittings for which were probably used by Lawrence for later portraits of George.

Caroline of Brunswick
by Sir Thomas Lawrence (detail)
Painted in 1804. Caroline, daughter of the
Duke of Brunswick, married the Prince of
Wales in 1795. It was a disastrous match,
and they separated after the birth of their
only child, Princess Charlotte, a year later.
Caroline died in 1821. She was never officially
recognised as queen.

sioned at Brighton. No expense was
spared, and craftsmen could more or less
name their own prices. Routine menus
carried more than a hundred dishes and
the spread on special occasions was enormous, imaginative and unforgettable.

George was an exhibitionist who
hurled himself into love affairs as into
politics, with a mixture of gushing praise
and tearful appeals. His guileless osten-
tation aroused furious resentment among
the shifting, embittered and dangerous
mass of the poor. Somebody even tried
to assassinate him. His wife, Caroline,
made George miserable, and they parted
in mutual loathing soon after the wedding. When he became king, Caroline
hastened back to England from self-
imposed exile to claim her inheritance.
An attempt to convict her of adultery
failed and George cowered away from
London while the mob there almost
rioted to show their support for her.

George was patently sincere and highly
intelligent, but hopelessly unsuited for
ruling a growing empire. He offended
public opinion by indulging in all the
pleasures of the flesh on an epic scale,
at a time when recovery after the war
with Napoleon and innovations in industry were causing enormous suffering
to his subjects. His immorality made a
sorry contrast to the domestic rectitude
of his father. Few remember him now
as a king, but as Regent he gave his name
to one of England's most celebrated
periods of architecture, furniture and
fashion.

George IV   *by Sir Thomas Lawrence*
This unfinished profile, said to have been
made for the coinage, probably dates from
c. 1814–15. Lawrence achieved early success
as a portrait painter, and his brilliance was
fully appreciated by the Prince Regent, for
whom he painted the great series of portraits,
now in the Waterloo Chamber at Windsor
Castle, of the sovereigns and statesmen
involved in the struggle against Napoleon.

(right)
George IV and the Duke of York
by George Crowhurst
There was a vogue for profile portraits in the
later eighteenth century, reflecting the
fashionable neo-classical taste, and they were
executed in wax, ivory, Wedgwood
medallions, and, above all, in silhouette.
Basically a tracing of a shadow, these could
be cut out of paper, or drawn or painted,
and being quick and cheap to make were
very popular. This 'confrontation' between
George IV (right) and the Duke of York is
by the profilist Crowhurst, who practised in
Brighton *c.* 1825–35.

William IV

Born 1765, reigned 1830–1837

The poet Shelley said that William and his brothers were 'the dregs of their dull race'; posterity has not hastened to rescue them from his judgement. William, third son of the Hanoverian George III, is perhaps the least known of British sovereigns of the past four hundred years. He is best remembered for being Queen Victoria's uncle. Like some of his successors in the twentieth century, he was a naval prince who rose to the rank of admiral of the fleet. But it was status rather than ability that elevated him. At the age of twenty-one William had been made captain of a frigate. He was so harsh that all his officers applied for transfers. Yet later he was ridiculed as 'Silly Billy' and became notorious for making rambling and intemperate speeches. He had no sense of proportion.

For more than twenty years before his marriage to Princess Adelaide, William lived with an actress, Mrs Jordan, who bore him ten children. When they separated she had little money and William was suspected of living off her earnings from the stage. He detested Victoria's mother and was desperate to live long enough for the princess to reach the age at which she could rule alone. He made it by less than a month.

William IV *by Reginald Easton*
In 1830, the year of his accession, Charles Greville wrote of this garrulous and choleric king, 'He seems a kind-hearted, well-meaning, not stupid, burlesque, bustling old fellow.' This water-colour was painted near the end of William's life. He wears the star, badge and sash of the Garter.

44

William IV when Duke of Clarence
by Sir Martin Archer Shee
A heroic portrait of William in the full-dress uniform of an admiral, painted around 1800, when Great Britain was at war with France. He is shown on a rocky sea-shore, with a cannon and draped flag beside him and a stormy sky behind. William's passion for the sea earned him the nickname 'Sailor Billy'.

Queen Adelaide *by Sir William Beechey*
Daughter of the Duke of Saxe-Coburg Meiningen, Adelaide married the Duke of Clarence, later William IV, in 1818. She shared his liking for a simple country life. This is a version of a full-length portrait painted soon after William's accession in 1830. Adelaide wears a dress of blue velvet with lace sleeves, and holds a spray of roses.

Victoria

Born 1819, reigned 1837–1901

If all other British sovereigns are ever forgotten, posterity will remember Queen Victoria. Her long reign is one of the neatest coincidences of history. When she came to the throne Britain had overcome the greatest power in Europe and was poised for a remarkable expansion of national achievement and wealth. Victoria was to preside over two-thirds of a century in which her kingdom was to progress with assurance to become for a brief and dazzling interval the most powerful nation on earth. There are people about today who lived when Britain viewed other nations in serene and satisfied isolation. In the last years of her reign no country could challenge the might of the Royal Navy, guardian of Britain's possessions overseas. Such was the destiny of the short, ardent and chubby princess who succeeded William IV. Victoria, the queen who gave her name to a culture, an era and the highest military decoration that her country could bestow, began her reign by ending Britain's royal link with Hanover. At the end of it she ruled a global empire 'on which the sun never sets'. Her life, grand in many of its aspects, was spectacular in its ironies. Her grandson was to preside as Kaiser Wilhelm II over the expansion of a rival power that was to corrode irreparably the confidence that had sustained Victorian Britain.

The queen was correct, dutiful, unpretentious, self-analytical and devoted to animals. She was the first British monarch to travel by train and the first to be photographed, mostly sitting gloomily in voluminous widow's weeds. After what she called a 'rather melancholy childhood' she fell in love with her 'excessively handsome' cousin, Albert, proposed to him and became a devoted wife and prolific mother. Her eldest child was the mother of the Kaiser, the next became King Edward VII, and the next was mother-in-law to the last Tsar. The present Queen is descended from Victoria through Edward VII, and the Duke of Edinburgh through her second daughter.

Victoria had nine children before the early death of her husband. Albert was a tireless worker who was worn down by the cares of government. He made Christmas trees popular in Britain and an early one, complete with candles and

Queen Victoria *by Aaron Penley*
A charming water-colour of the queen painted around 1840, the year of her marriage to Prince Albert, a bust of whom is seen beside her. The picture was purchased by the queen and then presented by her to the artist as a wedding present.

Queen Victoria *by Sir Francis Chantrey*
One of two drawings made with a 'camera lucida' (a method of projecting the outline of the face on paper by means of shadow), as a working study for Chantrey's marble bust of 1839 (see page 7). Over two hundred 'camera lucida' drawings by him are in the Gallery's collection.

The Royal Family
engraving by Samuel Cousins after the picture by Franz Xavier Winterhalter
Queen Victoria and Prince Albert are shown with their children, the Prince of Wales beside his mother, the Princess Royal and Princess Alice playing with the infant Princess Helena, and Prince Alfred on the left. The German-born Winterhalter was Queen Victoria's favourite artist, apart from Landseer, and this work, painted in 1846, was his most important commission from the English court. It cost £1000 and hung originally in the dining-room at Osborne House. Many of the royal portraits commissioned by Victoria and Albert stress the virtues of domesticity and family life.

Queen Victoria *by Sir George Hayter*
A replica of Hayter's coronation portrait of the young queen, weighed down by the crown and robes of state but gazing up with a look of girlish eagerness and idealism. Hayter was a favourite with the queen, and she described a small version of the portrait which he painted for her private apartments (now at Windsor) as 'excessively like and beautifully painted'. Hayter's other royal commissions included the big coronation group, the later marriage group and the christening of the Prince of Wales.

artificial snow, can be seen in a photograph taken at Windsor Castle more than 120 years ago. He was the instigator and principal organizer of the Great Exhibition of 1851, held in Hyde Park, which aimed to demonstrate Britain's supreme position among the nations of the world. Albert died of typhoid in 1861.

Bereavement plunged the queen into withdrawn widowhood which excited resentment and public criticism of the institution of monarchy itself. Victoria emerged from seclusion in time for her golden jubilee and lived beyond the celebration of its diamond successor. Her reign spanned immense social change, including enlargement of the franchise and the beginning of compulsory education. The queen witnessed huge strides in engineering and the growth of industry. Destiny ended her career with exquisite finesse only three weeks after the beginning of a century in which Victorian aims and attitudes were soon to become anachronisms.

Queen Victoria   *by Lady Julia Abercromby after Heinrich von Angeli*
A full-scale copy in water-colour of von Angeli's state portrait of 1875. Like the queen's earlier favourite, Winterhalter, von Angeli was German and he received many royal commissions. Lady Abercromby was one of the queen's ladies of the bedchamber, and a trained artist.

Queen Victoria   *by Mary Helen Carlisle*
A miniature, painted in water-colour on ivory. The original, of which this is a version, was purchased by Edward VII.

Prince Albert   *photograph by J. C. Mayall*
An informal and revealing image of Prince Albert taken at Osborne House on the Isle of Wight in August 1855. Albert's influence on Queen Victoria was immense. He was serious and industrious and keenly interested in scientific developments, the arts and social reform. He died in 1861, aged only forty-two.

Queen Victoria   *by Sir Edgar Boehm*
A terracotta head related to Boehm's
full-length statue of the queen outside
Windsor Castle, executed to commemorate
the 1887 jubilee.

Queen Victoria
woodcut by Sir William Nicholson
A well-known print executed at the time of
the Diamond Jubilee in 1897. It formed one
of a series of *Twelve Portraits*, commissioned
by W. E. Henley for the *New Review*. Its
homely imagery struck an immediate response
with the public.

The Four Generations
A photograph of Queen Victoria with the
Prince of Wales (later Edward VII), the Duke
of York (later George V), and the infant
Prince Edward (later Edward VIII), taken
by Chancellor of Dublin in 1899. The theme
of the four generations was a popular one
with royal photographers at this period.

Queen Victoria with an Indian attendant   One of the more endearing photographs of
the queen, working on state papers out-of-doors at Frogmore in 1891.

Edward VII

Born 1841, reigned 1901–1910

When the eldest son of Queen Victoria became king *The Times* commented with enormous tact: 'We shall not pretend that there is nothing in his long career which those who respect and admire him would wish otherwise'. Edward, the first British monarch to be crowned in the twentieth century, was very much a product of the nineteenth. For years he chafed as Prince of Wales against the rigorous attitude of his mother, who refused him any role in government. As king he showed himself a skilful and successful diplomatist, architect of the Entente with France which helped to end the 'splendid isolation' of the British empire. Early photographs of Edward show a bored, full sensuous face somewhat like that of his much more serious father, the Prince Consort. As Edward grew older he developed ever more bushy sideboards and beard until the familiar thick bush and plump physique of Edward the king appeared.

Edward is best known for a series of amorous liaisons that shocked his parents and revolted or amused his contemporaries. When no longer encumbered with the disapproval of his elderly mother Edward spiced his reign with a few years of high living that have had an irresistible appeal for subsequent generations. He loved sport, popular theatre and banquets of astounding size and richness. Whether dressed for the races or for some ceremonial in the uniform of a foreign regiment he liked to wear his hats at a rakish angle. He smoked thirteen fat cigars and twenty-two cigarettes a day. He had an easy manner and broad grin that helped to win new amorous contests when he was well over sixty. Many of his subjects loved their naughty, irrepressible and cheerful king. Years before, the Prince Consort had recognized that Edward lacked a profound intellect and had an insatiable appetite for novelty and diversion. Cars were one of his passions and he enjoyed speeding along the Brighton road.

Many people alive today can remember Edward's Britain, in which the gulf between rich and poor remained immense. Tum Tum, as the king was known, has given his real name to a period on which nostalgia has conferred the reputation of a vanished gaiety and sophistication. As Edward lay dying, almost the last news he heard of this world was that his horse had won at Kempton Park.

Edward VII when Prince of Wales
by George Frederic Watts
A drawing in coloured chalks related to a full-length portrait of Edward, commissioned by Lincoln's Inn around 1875. The finished oil portrait was exhibited in 1882, but the artist then took it back, as a result of criticism, and apparently destroyed it.

Queen Alexandra when Princess of Wales with her eldest sons, Prince Albert and Prince George (later George V)
photograph probably by George E. Hansen
One of a group of charming family photographs taken around 1874.

Edward VII when Prince of Wales
An anonymous photograph probably taken in the 1880s. It reveals him as a man of the world and a man of fashion.

Edward VII   *by Sir Luke Fildes*
A replica of the first official state portrait of Edward as king, presented to the Gallery by George V. The sitter is dressed in the uniform of a Field-Marshal, with an ermine mantle, holding a baton; the regalia are shown on the table beside him. The portrait follows the traditional imagery of state, in a somewhat leaden and derivative manner.

George V

Born 1865, reigned 1910–1936

When George V was a boy Queen Victoria gave him a watch for his birthday. She wanted it to remind him to be punctual and dutiful. As a youth he joined the Royal Navy and was tormented by his fellow cadets who knew that they were unlikely to have another chance to rag a prince of the blood royal. When he was twenty the old queen advised him to avoid 'races and betting and playing high'. Like his son George VI, he did not expect to become king and like earlier younger brothers of heirs apparent he was made Duke of York. But the Duke of Clarence, eldest grandson of Queen Victoria, died almost a decade before she did, and George had to exchange a naval career for that of potential successor to the throne. In 1891 Clarence became engaged to Princess May of Teck and in 1892 he died. In 1893 George married May and wrote soon afterwards: 'When I asked you to marry me I was very fond of you but not very much in love with you'. He soon was.

As king, George V was a nineteenth-century aristocrat faced with such twentieth-century phenomena as world war, socialist government and trade union un-

The Royal Family at Buckingham Palace
by Sir John Lavery
Painted in 1913 in the White Drawing Room, the picture depicts George V and Queen Mary with their two eldest children, the Prince of Wales (later Edward VIII) and the Princess Royal (later Countess of Harewood). The picture was commissioned by W. H. Spottiswoode for presentation to the nation, and it strikes an appropriately formal and grandiose note. Though the figures are a little like pasteboard, the treatment of the filtered, silvery light is a virtuoso performance.

George V when Duke of York
A studio photograph by the London Stereoscopic Company, taken around 1900.

George V and Queen Mary   *press photograph*
The king and queen are seen arriving for the opening ceremony at South Africa House in 1933. Characteristically, Queen Mary wears pale pastel colours and one of the toques for which she became well known.

Edward VIII   George VI

rest. He brought to the job of ruling a gigantic empire the austere sense of duty and lofty concern that he had learned as a young prince. He had no genius, but also no guile and no conceit. He reigned unopposed and celebrated a popular jubilee while his relatives, the last Kaiser and the last Tsar, were swept away. George and the latter were extraordinarily alike, with the same height, build and bushy naval beard. As Prince of Wales he went to India where 'I could not help noticing that the general bearing of the European towards the Native was, to say the least, unsympathetic'. As king he saw the rise of the first Labour Government: 'They have different ideas to ours as they are all socialists, but they ought to be given a chance'.

George V was a stern father who expected high standards in his own family. His gruffness was intensified by pain from injuries received from a rearing horse in the First World War. He died, a symbol of an earlier age, just before Hitler occupied the Rhineland.

Born 1894, reigned January–December 1936, died 1972

The most interesting and perhaps the most dangerous British monarch of the present century reigned for less than a year before he found the demands of kingship incompatible with the life he was determined to lead. As Prince of Wales he had been popular and lively, alarming his careful and correct father, George V. It was common knowledge before the old king died that Edward spent much of his time with Mrs Wallis Simpson, an American with one ex-husband still living. Soon after he succeeded, Edward, one of whose titles was Defender of the Faith, told his chief ministers that he intended to marry her whatever the consequences.

The country was enthralled by the drama of the abdication, and the king's final message was a poignant testimony to months of heart-searching. He told his myriads of subjects round the world: 'You must believe me when I tell you that I have found it impossible to carry the heavy burden of responsibility and to discharge my duties as King as I would wish to do, without the help and support of the woman I love'. To some he was a romantic hero, but to others he was Edward 'the Quitter', an erratic prince who evaded his duty.

Born 1895, reigned 1936–1952

Only eighteen months separated the births of Edward VIII and his brother George VI, but photographs give evidence of the differences between their personalities. The young Edward has an air of mischief while George, who felt eclipsed by him, looks serious and shy. The younger brother had a lonely and painful early life, unable to communicate with his father, George V, and allegedly damaged for years afterwards by the slapdash feeding of his nanny. Naval officers who examined him for entry into the service that absorbed a succession of princes said that he was the most nervous candidate they had ever seen. For years he had an intractable stammer and found official duties as Duke of York an ordeal. He was a devoted church-goer and Freemason. In the First World War George saw action at Jutland and later entered the Royal Naval Air Service where he became the first qualified pilot in the royal family. In peacetime he settled into a routine of tours abroad and visits at home, sustained by his wife, the Lady Elizabeth Bowes-Lyon.

George was appalled by the abdication. By a stroke of his brother's pen he was transmuted from a retiring and contented royal duke to 'George the Sixth, of Great Britain, Ireland and the British

Queen Mary   *press photograph*
Taken in 1939; the occasion is unknown. Tall and dignified, Queen Mary could appear austere, even formidable, but her strong sense of duty and service and her practical kindness won the nation's respect and affection. Art was one of her main interests (she was herself a collector), and she became an expert needlewoman. She died in 1953.

Edward VIII as Prince of Wales
photograph by Miss Edis
Taken at St James's Palace in 1920.

Edward VIII as Duke of Windsor
by Sir James Gunn
An attractive study for a group portrait of the Duke and Duchess of Windsor, painted in France in 1954.

Dominions beyond the seas; King and Emperor of India'. He, more than perhaps any other monarch, symbolises best the change in the international status of twentieth-century Britain. At his coronation he became ruler of countless millions, many of whom had never heard of him or of Britain. The Indian Empire alone contained not only modern India, but also Bangladesh, Burma and Pakistan. Barely more than a decade later Britain had been impoverished, the imperial power had been humbled at the fall of Singapore (1942) and the Indian Empire had forged its way to independence (1948).

George VI became a wise and respected statesman in his own right, experienced in foreign affairs and a potent focus of national pride in the Second World War. Like his father he had a strong sense of constitutional duty and was careful not to offend the post-1945 Labour Government, even though he was perturbed by some of its legislation. He told the Conservative Winston Churchill after the election in 1945 that the voters had been ungrateful. George died twenty years before the exiled brother who had abdicated in his favour.

George VI and Family at Windsor
photograph by Studio Lisa
Taken in 1940. Lisa and James Sheridan made their name with informal outdoor photographs of the royal family.

Queen Elizabeth, the Queen Mother
by Sir Gerald Kelly
Connected with Kelly's full-length state portrait of the Queen Mother, a pair with that of George VI, begun in 1939 and finally finished and exhibited in 1945.

George VI   *photograph by Walter Stoneman*
The date of this photograph is not known.

Conversation Piece at the Royal Lodge, Windsor   *by Sir James Gunn*
A perennially popular picture of the royal family. The figures are George VI, Queen Elizabeth, the Queen Mother, the present Queen and Princess Margaret. The scene is a tea-party at their favourite private residence, Royal Lodge; the date 1950. Though scarcely a great work of art, this meticulously rendered painting is a charming period piece. The portrait on the wall is of George IV by Lawrence.

51

Elizabeth II

Born 1926, succeeded to the throne 1952
The only British sovereign to be born in the twentieth century has faced the awesome task of reconciling her ancient and hallowed position with a society that favours earned against inherited wealth and admires the fruits gained by enterprise rather than by an accident of birth. The Queen has been supremely successful in winning the respect and affection of her subjects by devoting her life to their service. Elizabeth I presided over England's early ambitions beyond Europe and Victoria witnessed the zenith of her kingdom's power overseas. The first twenty-five years of Elizabeth II's reign have been marked first by a dismantling of the empire and then by the beginning of a new type of association in Europe. There are few monarchs left in the world and the Queen has managed better than most to combine regality with an unpretentious family life.

The Queen's ancestry can be traced, albeit by circuitous routes, back to William the Conqueror. She has less immediate power over her subjects than most of her predecessors had over theirs; she cannot imprison or exile a subject or embark on wars of her own. She lives a quiet family life and enjoys many of the same entertainments as her people. Yet in one sense she is forced to lead a life utterly remote from theirs. Hers is an inescapably public existence, much more so than that of any politician or pop star. The Queen is more permanent and more easily recognizable than they are. Nobody else in the land endures the same attention from constant crowds straining to see and to photograph. Her slightest gesture will be recorded and flashed round the world, a chance remark may excite wild speculation and the tiniest details of her everyday life arouse endless fascination and gossip. The Queen has been known to flinch, but no more than that, in the face of the role allotted to her.

Her Majesty the Queen and His Royal Highness the Duke of Edinburgh
photograph by Baron
A formal study, in the tradition of the grand state portrait, taken in April 1953 in the Green Drawing Room at Buckingham Palace. The Queen wears the ribbon and star of the Garter, and diamond jewellery. The brooch is a family heirloom, and the diadem, of considerable age, was re-set for Queen Victoria. The Duke of Edinburgh is in the uniform of Admiral of the Fleet.

Her Majesty the Queen and Queen Elizabeth, the Queen Mother   *press photograph*
Taken at Ascot in June 1963. The Queen shares her mother's keen interest in horse racing and other equestrian matters, and is herself an accomplished horsewoman.

(right)
Her Majesty the Queen   *by Pietro Annigoni*
The best-known portrait of the Queen, dating from 1954–55. Her Majesty is posed in Garter robes against a winter landscape. Annigoni combines a feeling for the Renaissance with brilliant realistic effects, and the portrait is both vivid and appealing as a likeness and striking in design.

Charles, Prince of Wales   *press photograph*
A photograph taken during the ceremonial
investiture of Charles as Prince of Wales by
Her Majesty the Queen, at Caernarvon Castle
in July 1969. Prince Charles is the twenty-first
bearer of a title customarily bestowed on the
eldest son of the sovereign since 1284, when,
according to tradition, Edward I presented
his son Edward, born at Caernarvon, to the
Welsh people as their prince. The crown,
made by Louis Osman and presented by the
Goldsmiths' Company, expresses ancient
symbolism through modern craftsmanship.

54

Her Majesty the Queen   *press photograph*
An informal photograph of the Queen, taken
in October 1965 at the North of Scotland
Gun Dog Association Retriever Trials on
Deeside.

Elizabeth had a retiring and rigidly
controlled childhood, for after the abdication of her uncle, Edward VIII, she
was in direct line of succession to the
throne. She never went to school, as her
children have done, and had no close
friends of her own age. She entered the
Second World War a shy and studious
teenager, having just met her future husband for the first time. She was thirteen
and he eighteen. Prince Philip, a distant
relative of the Queen through common
descent from children of Queen Victoria,
saw action at Cape Matapan and witnessed the surrender of Japan in Tokyo
Bay. Winston Churchill called their post-
war wedding 'a flash of colour on the
hard road they have to travel'. Prince
Philip got on well with his father-in-law,
George VI, and the young energetic
bridegroom with his characteristic long
stride would sometimes accompany the
dapper king on game-shooting expeditions. The young couple were on tour
in Kenya when George VI died and the
Princess became Queen Elizabeth II at
the age of twenty-five. She was already
the mother of two children, Prince
Charles, the heir to the throne, and
Princess Anne.

Elizabeth has since become triumphantly popular in many countries in
spite of criticism of herself, her money,
her interests and of the institution which
she represents. The Queen, now the
mother of four children, has been
described by the heir to the throne as
'terribly sensible and wise'.

The Royal Family
photograph by Desmond Groves
One of several group photographs taken in 1972 to celebrate the silver wedding of the Queen and Prince Philip. They are shown here with their four children: Prince Charles and Princess Anne standing beside their father, and seated by the Queen, Prince Edward (left) and Prince Andrew.

Her Majesty the Queen *by Pietro Annigoni*
Annigoni's second portrait of the Queen, painted in 1970. It was commissioned and presented to the Gallery by Hugh Leggatt. Her Majesty stands in an unearthly landscape, wearing the mantle of the Sovereign of the Order of the British Empire, with the Garter Star. The severe design of the portrait contrasts with the romantic spirit of Annigoni's earlier work, painted soon after the coronation.

Her Majesty the Queen *press photograph*
A charming photograph of the Queen, taken in December 1967 as she left Buckingham Palace to spend Christmas at Windsor Castle.

Her Majesty the Queen
photograph by Colin Davey
In July 1976, two hundred years after America's Declaration of Independence, the Queen arrives in Philadelphia at the beginning of her Bicentennial visit to the United States.

WILLIAM 1 ❧ Matilda

Robert, Duke of Normandy   WILLIAM 11   HENRY 1 ❧ (1) Matilda   Adela ❧ Stephen, Count of Blois
                                                     (2) Adela

William   Matilda ❧ (1) Emperor Henry V   STEPHEN
                           (2) Geoffrey Plantagenet
                              Count of Anjou

HENRY 11 ❧ Eleanor of Aquitaine

Henry   RICHARD 1 ❧ Berengaria   Geoffrey   JOHN   (1) Alice
                      of Navarre   (2) Avisa
                                                       (3) Isabella of
                                                           Angoulême

HENRY 111 ❧ Eleanor of Provence

EDWARD 1 ❧ (1) Eleanor of Castile
            (2) Margaret of France

EDWARD 11 ❧ Isabella of France

EDWARD 111 ❧ Philippa of Hainault

Edward, the ❧ Joan   Lionel, Duke ❧ Elizabeth   John of Gaunt ❧ (1) Blanche of Lancaster   Edmund, Duke ❧ Isabella   Thomas Duke
Black Prince   of Clarence   de Burgh   Duke of   (2) Constance of Castile   of York   of Castile   of Gloucester
                                             Lancaster   (3) Katherine Swynford

RICHARD 11 ❧ (1) Ann   Philippa ❧ Edmund   HENRY 1V ❧ Mary   John, Earl of   Edward, Duke   Richard, Earl ❧ Ann
            of Bohemia   Mortimer,   Bohun   Somerset   of York   of Cambridge   Mortimer
            (2) Isabella   Earl of March
              of Valois

Roger Mortimer ❧ Eleanor   HENRY V ❧ Catherine   John, Duke of   Richard, Duke ❧ Cecily
Earl of March   of France   Somerset   of York   Nevill

Edmund ❧ Ann ❧ Richard   HENRY VI ❧ Margaret   Margaret ❧ Edmund   EDWARD 1V ❧ Elizabeth   George ❧ Isabel   RICHARD 111 ❧ Ann
Mortimer   Mortimer   Earl of   of Anjou   Beaufort   Tudor   Woodville   Duke of   Nevill   Nevill
                    Cambridge   Clarence
(grandparents of EDWARD 1V)

Edward   HENRY V11 ❧ Elizabeth of York   EDWARD V   Richard Duke
                 (which united the Houses of York   of York
                        and Lancaster)

HENRY VII ❧ Elizabeth of York

Arthur, Prince ❧ Catherine of Aragon (1) ❧ HENRY VIII   Margaret ❧ James IV   Mary ❧ (1) Louis XII
of Wales   (2) Ann Boleyn   King of Scots   of France
                                      (3) Jane Seymour   (2) Charles Brandon
                                                                                     Duke of Suffolk

MARY I ❧ Philip II of Spain   EDWARD VI   ELIZABETH I   James V ❧ Mary of
                               (4) Ann of Cleves   King of Scots   Gulse
                               (5) Catherine Howard
                               (6) Catherine Parr   Mary, Queen of Scots ❧ Henry, Earl of Darnley

Ann of Denmark ❧ JAMES VI of Scotland, and 1 of England, Scotland & Ireland

Henry, Prince of Wales   CHARLES 1 ❧ Henrietta Maria   Elizabeth ❧ Frederick V King of Bohemia
                                      d. of Henry IV of France

CHARLES II ❧ Catherine   JAMES II ❧ (1) Ann Hyde   Mary ❧ William II   Sophia ❧ Ernest, Elector of Hanover
of Braganza   Mary of (2)   Prince of Orange
               Modena

James Edward,   MARY II ❧ WILLIAM III   ANNE ❧ George Prince   WILLIAM III ❧ MARY II   GEORGE I ❧ Sophia
the Old Pretender   of Denmark

GEORGE II ❧ Caroline of Anspach

Frederick, Prince of Wales ❧ Augusta of Saxe-Gotha

GEORGE III ❧ Charlotte of Mecklenburg-Strelitz

GEORGE IV ❧ Caroline of   Frederick, Duke   WILLIAM IV ❧ Adelaide of   Edward, Duke ❧ Victoria of Saxe-Coburg
Brunswick   of York   Saxe-Meiningen   of Kent

Charlotte   VICTORIA ❧ Albert of Saxe-Coburg

EDWARD VII ❧ Alexandra of Denmark

Albert, Duke of Clarence   GEORGE V ❧ Mary, Princess of Teck

EDWARD VIII   GEORGE VI ❧ Lady Elizabeth   Mary, Princess Royal   Henry, Duke of   George, Duke of Kent
               Bowes-Lyon   Gloucester

ELIZABETH II ❧ Philip, Duke of Edinburgh   Margaret ❧ Earl of Snowdon

Charles, Prince of Wales   Anne ❧ Mark Phillips   Andrew   Edward